IN SEARCH
OF THE
HIDDEN TREASURE

A Conference of Sufis

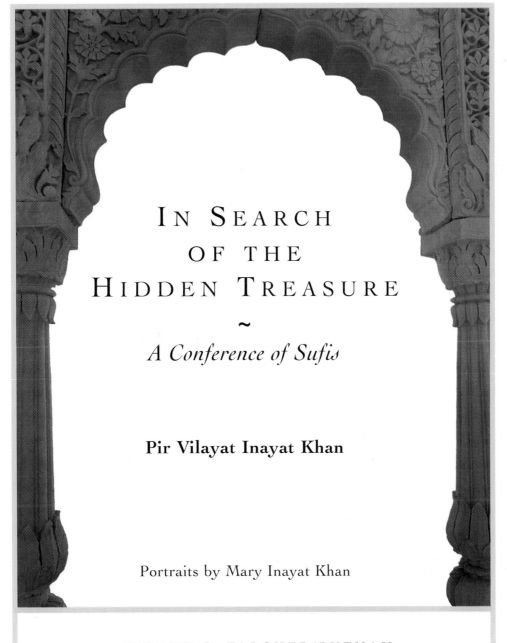

IN SEARCH
OF THE
HIDDEN TREASURE

~

A Conference of Sufis

Pir Vilayat Inayat Khan

Portraits by Mary Inayat Khan

JEREMY P. TARCHER/PUTNAM
A member of Penguin Putnam Inc.
New York

A BOOK LABORATORY BOOK

Most Tarcher/Putnam books are available at special quantity discounts for bulk purchase
for sales promotions, premiums, fund-raising, and educational needs. Special books or book
excerpts also can be created to fit specific needs. For details, write
Putnam Special Markets, 375 Hudson Street, New York, NY 10014.

JEREMY P. TARCHER/PUTNAM
a member of
PENGUIN PUTNAM INC.
375 Hudson Street
New York, NY 10014
www.penguinputnam.com

Produced by Book Laboratory Inc., Bolinas, CA
Designed by Victoria Pohlmann, New York, NY

Library of Congress Cataloging-in-Publication Data

IInayat Khan, Pir Vilayat.
    In search of the hidden treasure : a conference of Sufis / Pir Vilayat Inayat Khan:
portraits by Mary Vilayat Inayat Khan.
        p. cm.
    Includes bibliographical references (p.).
    ISBN 1-58542-180-4
1. Sufism. 2. Sufis. 3. Sufism — Study and teaching — History. I. Title.

BP189.I592 2003   2002075650
297.4 — dc21

Printed in the United States of America

10 9 8 7 6 5 4 3 2 1

Contents

Dedicated to my sister
Noor Inayat Khan,
Allied radio operator in World War II,
tortured to death at Dachau

PREAMBLE

Foreword

*I*n this uniquely conceived book, I present some of the key ideas and aphorisms of many of the better-known Sufi mystics of history. True to Sufi custom, I figure as a participant in this series of dialogues, and thus refer to my presence amongst the Sufi mystics in the third person. By conversing with the Sufi mystics and highlighting their understanding and experiences, we can discover clues to help illuminate reality as we search for meaningfulness.

In the dialogues I meet with a variety of inquirers and Sufi initiates, called "murids" (*muridan* in Persian), in order to grasp the vital subjects raised in the writings of Sufi dervishes. I interrogate these dervishes and sometimes interpret their statements by trying to reach into their minds and hearts, exploring unfamiliar dimensions of thinking to make them more accessible to the reader. To follow this dialogue, our minds must also reach beyond what is commonly accepted as the "here and now" in real space. In doing so we can enjoy dimensions of infinity in which our minds and hearts bridge the gap between the cosmic code and its actuation in the existential world. Moreover, we must account for the impact of our creativity in this existential dimension upon the universal code by dint of how we involve ourselves in the cosmic drama — even to the extent that we fashion our psyche and make states of realization corporeal.

I extrapolate upon and occasionally dramatize the aphorisms quoted here in novel or metaphorical ways. Wherever possible, I cite translated versions that are copied or paraphrased from existing publications, except where quotations are rendered from memory or interpreted or inferred freely. I have translated many of these quotations from French publications, although they may have appeared in more recent English publications. Except where otherwise noted, all quotations of Hazrat Inayat Khan are taken from the electronic database of his complete works.

The sequence of themes arising in this book describes the Sufi experience of the developmental stages of the seeker. Meditators wishing to conduct a retreat along Sufi principles could use *In Search of the Hidden Treasure* as a manual. It is a book to live with.

This book is a journey in the reader's mind through unfamiliar modes of thinking and emotions, across contradictions, complementarities, antinomies. It reconciles irreconcilables, paradoxes, and paradigms, and seeks to awaken the reader's mind from its singular perspective to another that is liberated from conditioned thinking.

In Search of the Hidden Treasure is not meant as an academic thesis. Instead, it is an attempt to connect the sayings of the Sufi dervishes, in the light of their earthly experience, with the queries and soul-searching of people in our day. The meetings are largely fictitious and do not represent the official view of any wing of Sufi thought.

Inspirational portraits of Sufis, painted by my wife Mary Inayat Khan, convey a sense of presence. They are impressions of the Sufi masters as the artist imagined them to be, except in cases where Mary was inspired by a previously existing portrait. The portrait of Hazrat Inayat Khan was made by Countess von Strachvitz. Illustrations from old manuscripts and publications are also reproduced in this book.

Since the Arabic words of the Qur'an lend themselves to a wide range of meanings and interpretations, I have selected the translations that confirm my own understanding of how they are interpreted by the Sufi dervish quoted.

Thanks are given here to Mariel Walters, Telema Hess, Dorothy Craig, Raqib Ickovits, Michael David Clarkson, Sharif Graham, Amida Cary, Yasodhara Sandra Lillydahl, Musawwira Butta, and Kerubiel Inayat Khan, who have helped edit the manuscript. The author particularly wishes to thank Jyoti Jessica Roshan and Melea Press for assisting him with the manuscript, and takes pleasure in giving special thanks to Aostra Hamman for her help with the references.

— Pir Vilayat Inayat Khan

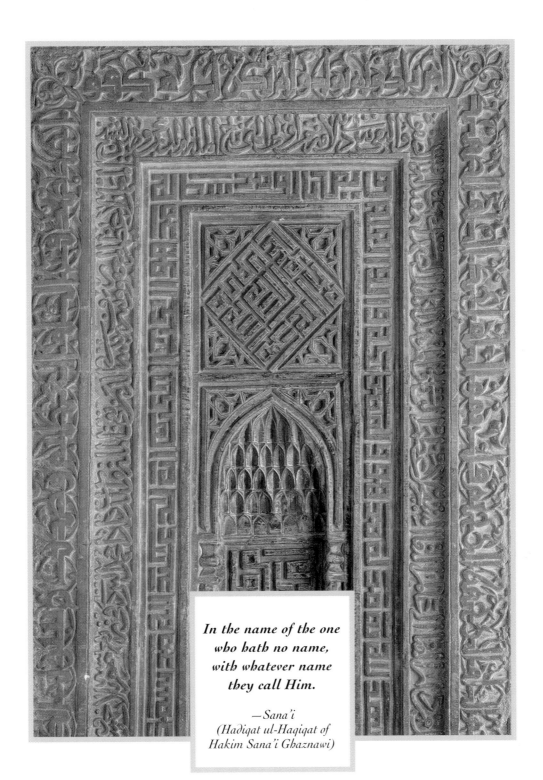

In the name of the one
who hath no name,
with whatever name
they call Him.

—Sana'i
(Hadiqat ul-Haqiqat of
Hakim Sana'i Ghaznawi)

MEETING BEYOND SPACE

MAULANA JALAL UD-DIN RUMI:

Happy the moment when we are seated in the palace,
  thou and I,

With two forms and with two figures but with one soul,
  thou and I.

The colors of the grove and the voices of the birds will
  bestow immortality

At the time when we shall come into the garden,
  thou and I.

The stars of heaven will come to gaze upon us:

We shall show them the moon herself, thou and I.

Thou and I, individuals no more, shall be mingled in
  ecstasy,

Joyful and secure from foolish babble, thou and I.

All the bright-plumed birds of heaven will devour their
  hearts with envy

In the place where we shall laugh in such a fashion,
  thou and I.

This is the greatest wonder, that thou and I, sitting here
  in the same nook,

Are at this moment both in Iraq and Khorasan, thou
  and I.

—Rumi, Maulana Jalal ud-Din. Rumi,
Poet and Mystic, translated by
Reynold A. Nicholson.

London: George Allan and Unwin Ltd., 1964.

Two dervishes meditating.

Falcon-shaped calligraphy of a prayer, Persia, early 19th century.

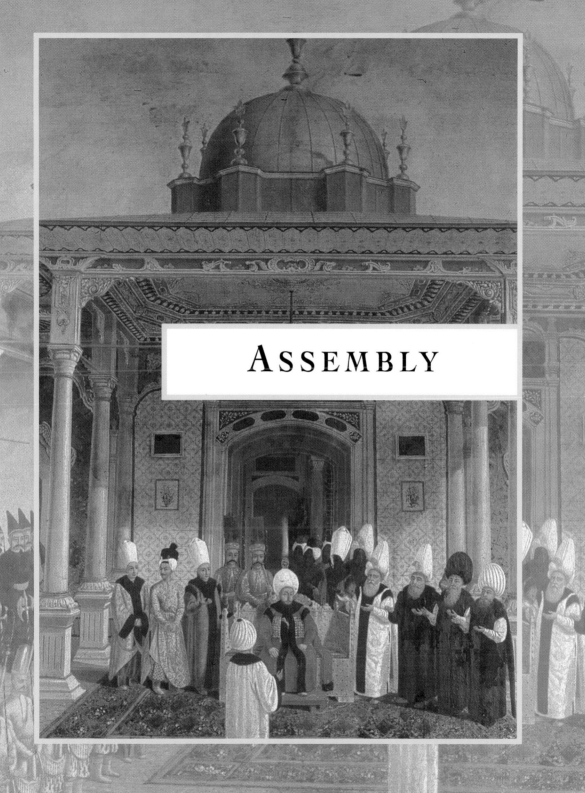

ASSEMBLY

THE GREAT ASSEMBLY OF SUFIS

Pir Vilayat Inayat Khan enters a hall filled with those who are inquiring about the Sufi path for the first time, as well as murids (Sufi initiates) who are familiar with the teachings. A sacred silence envelops the hall. Somehow the group is aware that it is not confined to the hall but is listening to a cosmic dialogue that transcends of space and time.

Crowned harpy—a creature from the world of dreams; 16th century woodcut.

PIR VILAYAT: What if the Sufis met not just beyond space but beyond time, in the sphere of metaphor called "Hurqalya," the world of dreams?

AN INQUIRER: Meeting beyond space and time sounds like pure metaphor or wishful thinking.

ANOTHER INQUIRER: Do you have any idea how to actually do this, to reach beyond space and time?

PIR VILAYAT: Yes. Imagine that while your body seems to be sitting in this hall, its aura has no boundary and its light hurtles into the starry sky. The walls of the hall are dispersing further and further into the galaxy. Not confined to space, your mind can reach into the minds of other beings, whose minds are likewise everywhere. It is dispersed in the galactic reaches, out of real time. So, envision that you are logging into a global conference in cyberspace and time, participating in a series of discussions with many dervishes. Perhaps you will ask the same questions that other inquirers and murids are asking, or the dervishes will answer your unspoken questions. The human mind enjoys wandering in other dimensions where it escapes being forcibly fitted into the simplistic logical patterns of the commonplace thinking of our ancestral civilizations, which pigeonholes human experience into discrete categories.

Woodcut of astronomers observing moon.

Just ponder:
We can see today stars
That no longer exist,
That have disintegrated many thousand
light-years ago.
Furthermore,
Events in the starry cosmos
Can only be seen
As occurring simultaneously
When perceived
From a local vantage point.

INQUIRER: This is mind boggling!

PIR VILAYAT: Yes, it challenges our minds to burst forth beyond the edges of our accustomed worldview. It frees us from the constraints of the commonplace space-time framework.

ANOTHER INQUIRER: Is this what happens to our minds when we meditate?

PIR VILAYAT: In meditating, we explore unfamiliar dimensions that one might call inner space. The universe is constantly refashioning itself as me in the measure of my realization of its meaningfulness to me. Through my inventiveness it discovers new potentialities hitherto unknown, just as in music variations on a theme bring out the richness potentially present in the theme. I imagine God as a cosmic musician exploring new attunements in His emotion through the jubilations, afflictions, and distresses in our hearts.

Imam calling the faithful to prayer.

While pondering their soul-searching by logging into cyberspace, those present at the assembly are hearing echoes of the litanies of imams (prayer leaders) and dervishes reciting verses of the Qur'an from mosques throughout the world, resonating with the queries arising in the great hall.

MEETING BEYOND TIME

MURID: Could you give me some idea as to how the mind grasps things in the state of meditation?

PIR VILAYAT: As our mind takes wing beyond the fragmented mode of existential thinking and explores transcendent modes of thinking, it grasps interconnections instead of categories. Precisely as modern physicists do, the mind perceives a nonlocal, acausal relationship between events — synchronicity rather than linearity. This mode of thinking is very challenging to our conditioned habits of thinking and sparks a sense of freedom and bliss.

In these explorations into meaningfulness, can you see that our commonplace notions of time are totally inadequate and stand in the way of our understanding the cosmic process in which we are involved? As soon as you grasp that there are dimensions of time beyond the linear process of becoming, which we call the

Sculpture from the Seljuq citadel of Konya, Turkey.

"arrow of time," the perspectives that those who inspire us, the Sufis, have opened come to light.

INQUIRER: I have heard about mysterious mystics, sometimes called "Sufis," sometimes "dervishes." Could you describe them and tell us something about their thoughts? Do they make sense to you?

PIR VILAYAT: [Laughs.] It is only possible to understand what they are saying by pressing your thoughts beyond your ordinary reach. The only way to understand them is to dare to imagine how things would look from the point of view opposite your own — the antipodal vantage point — which the Sufis call the "divine point of view."

Scenes from the Khamsah of Amir Khusrau.

ANOTHER INQUIRER: Can we really do that?

PIR VILAYAT: Let us imagine that our minds are able to log into their minds and theirs into ours, so that it is not important when they lived or where they are. Our simplistic minds would like to imagine them gathering in an assembly somewhere, but they can meet in cybernetic space-time. Just imagine that they can communicate without being in the same place. Imagine the electrons of their bodies scattered after death yet still relating nonlocally. Likewise, imagine that their minds are able to communicate as in telepathy: They can listen in to conversations, or interject when their point of view is being discussed, even parading in their erstwhile attires or demeanors. What is more, imagine that they can communicate with us and answer our questions, shifting from the timeless and spaceless into the "here and now" and spiriting away again. They are unbounded by our commonplace way of reducing the outreach of human thought to a framework of three-dimensional space and one-dimensional time.

MURID: Would the meditative thinking that you are talking about give us a clue as to whether we can continue thinking without a body after death?

The Alhambra, Granada, Spain.

PIR VILAYAT: Perhaps the mind, in its ability to project metaphor, discovers a cryptic reality that opens clues to the ubiquitous unknown. [Pauses.] Can you envision yourself as the prow of the forward march of evolution — the whole past of the universe striving to move forward, verging onto new horizons?

MURID: Do you think we could actually ask the mystics questions?

PIR VILAYAT: Shall we venture?

Selim III granting audience at the Gate of Felicity, 18th century painting in the Topkapi Museum, Istanbul.

An innumerable host of Sufi pirs, dervishes, saints, and murids fills the hall whose walls are dispersed in outer space. They begin intoning a Sufi mantra (ism ilahi): "Ya Jami (God, O Gatherer)."

Hazrat 'Ali

Hazrat 'Ali, the son-in-law of Prophet Muhammad and his appointed successor, opens the great assembly of Sufis in the far reaches of the unknown with the Islamic invocation Fatiha:

Bismillah ir-rahman ir-rahim;
Alhamdu li-llahi rabb il'alamin;
ar-rahman ir-rahim;
Maliki yaum id-din;
Iyyaka na'budu wa iyyaka nasta'in;
Ihdina's-sirat al-mustaqim;
Sirat aladhina an'amta 'alayhim
Ghayri'l-maghdubi 'alayhim
Wa la'd-dalin.

(In the name of God, magnanimous
and compassionate,
Glory to God, Sovereign of all worlds,
Magnanimous and compassionate,
Master of the day of requital,
Thee alone do we worship, and from
Thee alone do we implore help.
Guide us on the straight path,
The path of those to whom Thou hast
accorded Thy grace,
Not that of those who have incurred
Thy wrath,
or of those who have gone astray.)

AN INQUIRER: [Posing a question to the gathering of Sufis.] For believers, prayers like this come naturally, but I can only rely on my own experience. Are believers not praying to a being who is a projection of their imagination?

ANOTHER INQUIRER: I cannot understand how anyone could simply assume the existence of God without any proof! How can one affirm that this hypothetical being is endowed with omniscience — and how can one presume to know what She knows?

PIR VILAYAT: Could you accept that the cosmos, as it extends in interstellar, intergalactic space, is one entity, at once fragmented and whole?

ONE MURID, A SCIENTIST: According to the holistic paradigm in science, for example, when a crystal is fractured each fragment behaves like the whole crystal. By the same token every fragment, every fragment of the cosmos potentially carries the code of the universe.

PIR VILAYAT: Do you not think that as a whole, the universe is endowed with a global mode of thinking, emotion, intelligence, consciousness, will?

INQUIRER: This way of considering reality is different from our anthropomorphic representation of God as a being.

PIR VILAYAT: Can you conceive of the cosmos — including all the galaxies, Planet Earth, and human bodies — as the body of that global reality we call the universe?

INQUIRER: Yes, I can appreciate the difference you are making between the universe and the cosmos.

MURID: Can we have any idea of what the thinking of the universe might be?

PIR VILAYAT: Yes. We could illustrate it thus: We do not know whether our nerve cells have any idea of the thinking of the brain that they serve. Does not the sensitivity of the fingers of a violinist, though, reveal clues as to how the brain thinks? If the universe is one global reality, do you not think that our thoughts are part of that global thinking? Do you not think that our thinking contributes to the global thinking? Do you not think that our thoughts can infer clues as to that global thinking?

INQUIRER: Yes, if you put it that way.

Lion formed of ornamental Tawqi script which translates as:
Ali ibn Abi Talib, may God Almighty be pleased with him
and honor him. Persia, probably 19th century.

GOD–A PROJECTION

An Indian pir-o-murshid, Hazrat Inayat Khan, emerges from the twentieth century. In the style of his Indian predecessors, he is clad in a golden robe adorned with a winged heart. He seems to carry upon his shoulders the souls of thousands of murids from Europe and America. A late arrival, he takes immediate delight in the company of ecstatic Sufis present.

Hazrat Inayat Khan

MURID: *O Murshid* (teacher), you are here! Do you remember me? I was your *murid*. You changed my life!

HAZRAT INAYAT: The *murshid* is there for the *murid*. That is his reason for being.

The effigy of Khwaja Mu'in ud-Din Chishti, founder of the Chishti Order entered in Ajmer, India, seems to adumbrate his presence. (The Sufis not only concentrate on their great predecessors, but imagine how it would be to be them. Therefore, there is a belief that the predecessors' semblance can be perceived through their effigies).

HAZRAT INAYAT: [To inquirers.] Let me answer your earlier questions: The man who has no imagination to make a God, and is not open to a conception of God (even his own), finds no stepping stone to reach the knowledge that his soul longs for but that his doubts deny.[1] No one who has been unable to make a representation of God has ever reached God. So far there has only been a belief in God. God exists in people's imagination as an ideal. Believing is the first step. By this process the God within is awakened and made living. It is in those who are God-conscious that God becomes a reality so that He is no longer an imagination....If there is

Khwaja Mu'in ud-Din Chishti

any sign of God to be seen, it is in the God-conscious. It is in man that the divine perfection can be seen. Man brings to the world a living God, who without it would remain in the heavens.[2]

INQUIRER: Is it not wishful thinking to imagine God as a great being endowed with a personality?

HAZRAT INAYAT: People ask, "If all is God, then God [cannot be] a person." The answer: Though the seed does not show the flower in it, yet the seed culminates in the flower, and therefore the flower already existed in the seed. No doubt it would be a great mistake to call God a personality, but to deny the personality of God is an even-greater mistake....[3] It is not wrong to make God in one's imagination the God of all beauty, for by that imagination one is drawn nearer and nearer every moment of one's life to that divine ideal which is the seeking of one's soul.... Man, in the flowering of his personality, expresses the personality of God.[4]

> *The gathering can hear the Sufi dervishes*
> *at the mosque in Mecca*
> *repeating a* hadith *(statement) of the Prophet:*
> *"*Man 'arafa nafsahu faqad 'arafa rabbahu
> *(Whosoever knows himself knows his Lord)."*

PIR VILAYAT: In order to imagine God, the faithful project what they think God to be, ascribing to Him qualities that they observe in their personalities, in those of others, or in perceptual phenomena — qualities that are represented in their minds as perfect. Our mind is equipped with the ability to represent to itself qualities as perfect as it can imagine. The mind calls these qualities "divine attributes."

HAZRAT INAYAT: God is hidden within His creation. Awaken the God within. It is in man that divinity is awakened, that God is awakened, that God can be seen.

ANOTHER MURID: To know God must I imagine God? Is that not also wishful thinking?

HAZRAT INAYAT: Man can reach God only as far as his imagination can take him.[5] Make God as great and as perfect as your imagination can. By making God great we ourselves arrive at a certain greatness; our vision widens, our thought deepens, our ideals reach higher. We create a greater vision, a wider horizon, for our own expansion. By way of prayer, by praise, by contemplation, we should therefore imagine God as great as we possibly can.[6]

SHAYKH MUHYI UD-DIN IBN 'ARABI: [Responding as from an unreachable distance.] To Him we attribute no quality without ourselves having that quality.[7]

PIR VILAYAT: By doing so, the faithful arouse in their prayer dormant qualities in themselves, modeling them upon their representation of how these qualities would be if they were perfect, thus fostering personal growth. Thus prayer is itself the ultimate creative act.

MURID: [To Pir Vilayat.] Are you saying that to fashion our personality we need to match the qualities in our psyche, such as they are, with archetypes that represent a higher dimension of our being?

PIR VILAYAT: Yes. We tend to consider what is really the transcendent dimension of our being to be what we mean by God. The famous Sufi Shaykh Ibn 'Arabi and many others consider that if we apply the holistic paradigm, all beings are intermeshed in the cosmic web — the universe. Here infinite and finite are two incommensurable poles, just as the number one is incommensurable with infinity. The Islamic prayer is a dialogue between the supplicant in her personal identity and God as the supplicant imagines God to be. The supplicant tries to see herself from the antipodal vantage point — as she envisions God seeing her. Prayer, then, is a dialogue between two poles of ourselves rather than between two separate entities.

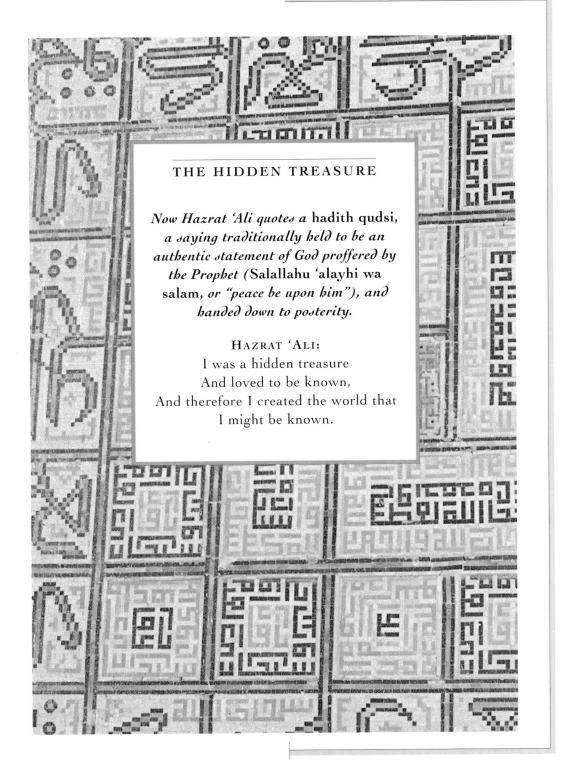

THE HIDDEN TREASURE

Now Hazrat 'Ali quotes a hadith qudsi, *a saying traditionally held to be an authentic statement of God proffered by the Prophet* (Salallahu 'alayhi wa salam, *or "peace be upon him"), and handed down to posterity.*

HAZRAT 'ALI:
I was a hidden treasure
And loved to be known,
And therefore I created the world that
I might be known.

TO BE KNOWN

Shaykh ul-Akbar
Muhyi ud-Din ibn ʻArabi

With an air of great eminence, the Shaykh ul-Akbar (Great Shaykh) Muhyi ud-Din ibn ʻArabi, arrayed in his magnificent silver burnoose and surrounded by a school of learned scholars, formulates his commentary on the hadith *recited by Hazrat ʻAli.*
Following the custom of the Sufis, his magnificent countenance was adumbrated by the effigy of Khidr, depicted by the Muslims as the green phantom that appears to wanderers lost in the desert and guides them to safety.

IBN ʻARABI: One could say: God wished to see His own essence in a global object that, being endowed with existence, summarized the divine order so that He may thus manifest His mystery to Himself.[8]

MURID: This sounds paradoxical. What do Sufis mean by "essence"?

PIR VILAYAT: Sufis make a difference between the world and what lies beyond, which they call the essence.

ANOTHER MURID: What does Ibn ʻArabi mean by the "divine order" of the universe?

PIR VILAYAT: The code beyond existence — that is, the possibilities that are actuated (realized) in existence. In order to discover what possibilities lie latent, God becomes in every consciousness the knowing subject. God becomes in each of our personalities the object of Her self-discovery.

OUT OF LOVE?

PIR VILAYAT: [To murid.] Did you notice that the hadith said, "I loved to be known," not "I wished to be known"?

MURID: I thought I understood that it was in order to know Himself that God created creation?

Now Maulana Jalal ud-Din Rumi, the great Sufi mystic-poet who introduced the dervish whirling-step to echo the choreography of the stars, comes forth, bursting with overwhelming conviction as though to make a momentous statement.

Maulana Jalal ud-Din Rumi

RUMI: On the Day of Alast, the Beloved said something else in a whisper. Do any of you remember? He said, "I have hurried to you." [9]

Pir Vilayat comes forth again, exulted by the magical scene.

PIR VILAYAT: You see, you see! The hidden treasure not only desires to be known, but aspires to become in the course of evolution the *Dhu'l-Jalal wa'l-Ikram*, the Lord of Majesty and Power!

MURID: [To Rumi.] Are you inferring that the moving impulse behind creation was not knowing, but love? Could we infer therefore that love for our fellow beings spurs our quest for knowledge?

RUMI: The creatures are set in motion by love.[10]

The question echoes in the vastness of outer space, reaching the minds of the faithful at the Mosque of Konya, Turkey. The imam of the mosque recites, "He will love them and they will love Him." (Qur'an 5:59)

Rumi kneels in prayer.

MURID: Can you tell us what you are experiencing?

RUMI:
I asked: "Who art thou?"
He said, "The desire of all."
I asked: "Who am I?"
He said, "The desire of the desire." [11]

If there had not been a desire and hope for the fruit, why did the gardener plant the tree? The branch came into existence for the sake of the fruit. Although the fruit comes last into existence, it is first, because it is the goal. [12]

Fabulous beasts, drawing of the Turkoman School.

HAZRAT INAYAT: The whole of manifestation is just like a tree sprung from the divine root, and from this tree the same seed is produced — the human soul — which was the first cause of the tree. The seed, which is the origin of the flower and the fruit, is also the result of the flower and the fruit. The seed comes last, after the life of trunk, branch, fruit, and flower. Just as the seed is sufficient in itself and capable of producing another plant, so man is the product of all the planes, spiritual and material, yet in him alone shines forth that which caused the whole — that primal intelligence, the seed of existence — God. [13]

MURID: So, did God create humanity to know Himself or out of love?

PIR VILAYAT: You see, there are two dimensions to this *hadith qudsi*. For those seeking understanding, the divine motivation to create the world was for God to know Himself by projecting Himself as the object perceived, the world. But then there is the covert realization of the mystic, to which Maulana Jalal ud-Din Rumi refers: the Sufi way

DNA model—a divine plan.

of the heart. God descended from the solitude of unity, in the state of ama (the inscrutable cloud beyond our understanding), where He knows Himself in the principles of His being, out of love for the possibility of you, of us. Thereby, His transcendent prototype was elaborated in our understanding just as we define an archetype by giving a number of diverse exemplars. By bringing to light God's potential bounty, God added a further mode of knowledge to the knowledge that He entertained in the seedbed of existence, where the dichotomy of lover and beloved had not yet emerged out of the state of unity.

The Sufi dervish Mansur Hallaj, lost in divine love, interjects from his state of meditation.

HALLAJ: By dint of a thought among His thoughts, God turned toward the thought of unreciprocated love in the solitude of the original oneness.[14]

A beautiful, powerful voice echoes through the assembly, as the female Sufi saint Rabi'a 'Adawiyya repeats a second hadith *of the Prophet.*

'ADAWIYYA: But for thee I would not have created the heavens.

SHAYKH FARID UD-DIN 'ATTAR: O God, it is because of Thy nostalgia that I am on earth and my nostalgia, that I resurrect.[15]

The imam of the Mosque of Mecca recites, "I cast the garment of love over thee from Me, and this in order that thou mayest be reared under Mine eye." (Qur'an 20:39)

Rabi'a 'Adawiyya

SECRET BECAUSE SACRED

MURID: You still have not told me how the hidden treasure that loves to be known can be known by us!

IBN 'ARABI: The Real is greater and more exalted than that He should be known in Himself.[16] However, our intelligence can convey some kind of receptivity beyond rational thinking.[17]

All of a sudden, a strange, terrifying man blows in from the desert
— quizzical, perplexing, intoxicating beyond measure.
His voice speaks the voice of wilderness, his gaze is the gaze of the far
reaches of the mind. It is 'Abd ul-Jabbar Niffari.

'Abd ul-Jabbar Niffari

NIFFARI: God warned me, "Thou mayest not," and again, "Thou mayest not," and again seventy times: "Thou mayest not describe how thou seest Me, nor how thou enterest My treasury, nor how thou takest from it My seals through My power, nor how thou seekest the knowledge of one letter from another letter through the might of My magnificence."[18]

IBN 'ARABI: For it is not possible for the door to the invisible world and its secrets to be opened while the heart craves for them.[19]

HAZRAT INAYAT: It is owing to our limitation that we cannot see the whole being.[20] But it is the nature of the soul to try and discover what is behind the veil; it is the soul's constant longing to climb beyond its power; it is the desire of the soul to see something that it has never seen; it is the constant longing of the soul to know something it has never known. But the most wonderful thing is that the soul already knows there is something behind this veil of perplexity; that there is something to be sought for in the highest spheres of life; that there is some beauty to be seen; that there is Someone to be known who is knowable. This desire, this longing, is not acquired; this desire is a dim knowledge that soul has in itself.[21]

HALLAJ (portrait on page 141): O consciousness of my consciousness, so subtle that it escapes the imagination of all living beings.[22]

CONCEALED / REVEALED

MURID: Why does it have to be secret?

HAZRAT INAYAT: It is secret because it is sacred and therefore needs to be protected. If we could ever grasp things as seen from the divine mind, we would be shattered.

PIR VILAYAT: This secret is trying to reveal itself to you, but you would be so overwhelmed if you were to discover the magnitude of your real being in the universe. Therefore you are being protected from that knowledge until you are ready for it.

NIFFARI: God said, "I am the manifester of the manifestation unto that which, if it were to appear unto it, would consume it."[23]

Ibn 'Arabi's mind now suddenly attunes to the dervishes in their prayers. He kneels.

IBN 'ARABI: How can I know Thee since Thou art hidden, unknown to me? How could I fail to know Thee since Thou art that which appears and all things make Thee knowable to me?[24] When He discloses Himself there is no other; when He conceals Himself, everything is other.[25]

Maulana 'Abd ur-Rahman Jami, Iran's renowned poet, joins in.

JAMI: Glory be to Him who hides Himself by the manifestations of His light and manifests Himself by drawing a veil over His face.[26]

PIR VILAYAT: God, the hidden treasure, is concealed behind the very veil that reveals Him and reveals Him by the very veil that conceals Him.

IBN 'ARABI: Thou hast veiled Thyself from the glances and Thou hast eluded Thyself from the perception of intelligences; but Thou hast revealed Thyself by the manifestation of the properties of Thy attributes; and thus unfurl themselves the hierarchies of existence.[27]

'Abd ur-Rahman Jami

INQUIRER: On one hand you Sufis say that God desires or loves to be known. On the other hand you say He is a secret treasure. How can God both wish to be known and hide Himself?

IBN 'ARABI: One may see the Real behind the veil of things. Things are like curtains over the Real. When they are raised, unveiling takes place.[28]

Maulana 'Abd ul-Karim Jili, the noble metaphysician
(portrait on page 106), joins the dialogue.

JILI: Know that with regard to yourself you are thus simultaneously manifested and hidden to yourself.[29]

HALLAJ: [To murid.] No one knows Him except the one to whom He makes Himself known.[30]

The voice of the imam of the Shahjahani Jama' Masjid
in Delhi echoes in the assembly:
"He revealed to His servant what He revealed."
(Qur'an 53:10)

IBN 'ARABI: [Interpreting.] He does not disclose Himself to you except to the measure that your level of realization allows.[31]

INQUIRER: What do you mean by "level of realization"?

PIR VILAYAT: Imagine that you are pursuing an achievement that you have planned carefully, and your daughter asks why you are doing this or that. It is likely that she is not ready to understand your planning, and any explanation that you might give may well be misconstrued. If she should act upon her imperfect understanding she might damage, even cause havoc to, your plans. However, the further the child matures the more of your intention you can reveal to her. This is what is meant by awakening — awakening to the divine programming.

JAMI: Viewed in His aspect of multiplicity and plurality, under which He displays Himself when clothed with phenomena, God is the whole created cosmos. Therefore, the cosmos is the outward visible expression of the Real and the Real is the inner reality of the cosmos.[32]

PIR VILAYAT: One's true being is hidden behind many veils that scramble it in a jumble of superimposed images. The deeper features of one's being are distorted by the games of the ego passing through the peripheral layers. But the core — the hidden treasure — is immaculate. The only way to grasp the immaculate core of one's being to see into the depth of who one truly is, is to reverse the distortions, to purify oneself by the power of authenticity.

'ATTAR: [To Jami.] In this world, you have crossed several veils in order to penetrate through the perceptible to that which is beyond the perceptible.[33]

ESPY HIM EVERYWHERE

Dhu'n-Nun Misri, an Egyptian dervish, speaks.

MISRI:
O God!
I never hearken
To the voices of the beasts
Or the rustle of the trees,
The splashing of waters
Or the song of birds,
The whistling of the wind
Or the rumble of thunder,
But I sense in them
A testimony to Thy unity.[34]

All that the eyes behold
Belongs to earthly knowledge,
But that which the heart beholds
Is true knowledge.[35]

Dhu'n-Nun Misri

Roof of an Imamzadah in Kashan, Iran.

Baba Kuhi

An ecstatic majdhub *(one lost in God) from Shiraz (Iran), Baba Kuhi, echoes that exclamation.*

BABA KUHI:

In the market, in the cloister, only God I see.
In the valley, on the mountains, only God I see.
In favor, in misfortune, only God I see.
In prayer, in contemplation, in fasting, only God I see.
When I looked with God's eyes, only God I saw.[36]

The beloved Turkish poet Yunus Emre recites some of his verses.

EMRE:

With the mountains, with the stones
Will I call Thee, Lord, O Lord!
With the birds in early dawn
Will I call Thee, Lord, O Lord!

With the fishes in the sea,
With gazelles in the deserts free,
With the mystic's call "O he!"
Will I call Thee, Lord, O Lord![37]

JAMI:

Neighbor and associate and companion—
Everything is He.
In the beggar's coarse frock and in the
    king's silk—
Everything is He.
In the crowd of separation,
And in the loneliness of collectiveness,
By God—everything is He.[38]

Miniature of Sufi poet, Yunus Emre.

The imam of the shrine of Sayyida Nafisa in Cairo is repeating, "Wherever you turn is the face of God." (Qur'an 2:115)

Hazrat Inayat is moved to recollect his own experience.

HAZRAT INAYAT: Every form I see is Thine own form, my Lord. In every place I feel Thy presence, Beloved. When I close my eyes in the solitude, I see Thy glorious vision in my heart; and, opening my eyes amid the crowd, I see Thee acting on the stage of the earth. Always I am in Thy dazzling presence, my Beloved. Thou takest me to heaven, and Thou bringest me on earth in the twinkling of an eye.[39]

Khwaja Baha ud-Din Naqshband, the founder of the Naqshbandi Order who taught God-consciousness, is surrounded by chanting dervishes.

KHWAJA NAQSHBAND: *Hosh dar dam, nazar bar qadam, khilwat dar anjuman!* (Be conscious of your breath and watch every step you take, and thus experience solitude in the crowd!)[40]

The dervishes chant, "Hama ust (Everything is he)."

Khwaja Naqshband

MAYA — DELUSION

Abu Yazid Bastami, an austere dervish hailing from the deserted mountains of Northern Iran, blows in like a storm, dressed in ignominious rags. Having contained itself a long time, his vehemence knows no bounds.

Abu Yazid Bastami

BASTAMI:
Khada! Khada! Ya Muakhir!
Khada! Khada! Ya Muakhir!
(Hoax, hoax! O deceiver! O leader astray!)

When God reveals Himself to the sages, in an initial stage, He shows them a market in which only effigies of men and women are on sale; those who venture in this market will never visit God. Oh, God beguiles thee, not only in this market but also in that of the next world![41]

The imam of the mosque of Baghdad intones,
"God is the best of devisers." (Qur'an 3:54)

INQUIRER: (Yelling, outraged.) I cannot imagine God as a deceiver! You Sufis call Him the truth, even the very paragon of truth!

PIR VILAYAT: We know that what appears to our understanding is often quite deceptive. But it is not good enough to say that, because we wish to know how things are in reality. Islam presents a positive note that complements rather than contradicts the theory of *maya* (illusion).

JAMI: The world is an illusion, but reality eternally manifests through it.[42]

HAZRAT INAYAT: Unreality will not prove satisfactory in the end, because satisfaction lies in the knowledge of truth. For the time being, if unreality satisfies one — to think that [all existence] is real — one may continue to think in that way. But it must be said that in the end this will not prove to be real. In order to avoid future disappointment, one must find it out soon in one's life if one is to be capable of grasping and then assimilating the ultimate truth....[43] How can one attain truth? In order to attain truth one must make one's own life truthful.... But it is most difficult to practice this moral in this world of falsehood, where every move one makes is touched by some unreality. Every moment of a person's life is touched by falsehood likely to [influence] him.[44]

The Imam of the mosque at the **Dargah** *(Tomb) of Mashhad*
recites an **ayah** *(verse) from the Qur'an: "God shows His signs in*
nature and in the human soul." (Qur'an 41:53)

IBN 'ARABI: [To Bastami.] The signs alert us to what they manifest, what they reveal. He is known through things.[45]

The Sufi dervishes at the Dargah of Shaykh ibn 'Arabi in
Damascus, Syria, are repeating a verse of the Qur'an:
"Everything will perish except His countenance."
(Qur'an 28:86) *

IBN 'ARABI: Thou knowest the world in the degree of which one can know the shadows; and thou art ignorant of God in the degree of thy ignorance of the person on whom this shadow depends. [46]

Subtly adorned and perfumed after the high tradition of Iranian poets, and with music in his voice, Farid ud-Din 'Attar offers his services as a wise counselor to the assembly.

'ATTAR: Surely that hoax that so grieves Abu Yazid Bastami is a protection. The annals of the history of Iran have recorded the case of a potentate so magnificent that some of his subjects would pass out as he processed in royal pomp in the yearly parade. To protect his subjects against the glare of his splendor, he wore a veil. [47]

PIR VILAYAT: But by some great paradox, the very veil whereby He conceals Himself to protect us reveals Him to us in the measure of our capacity to espy in its contours the features of the divine face.

MURID: What does the hadith recited by the Imam of the Dargah of Mashhad mean by "signs"?

Mosque of the Haram, Mecca.

PIR VILAYAT: The beauty of a sunrise in the high mountains, of a crystal, of a flower. A lovely or expressive face, a compassionate gesture, a sublime work of art, magnificent music, the inspirational lore of a poet. All are clues that might lead us to espy the splendor and intelligence behind all of this, the splendor that is trying to reveal itself to us.

Echoes are reaching the assembly from the congregation at the Ka'aba reciting an ayah in its prayers: "Whither you turn, there is the face of God."
(Qur'an 2:115)

IBN 'ARABI: Since the ephemeral being manifests the form of the eternal, it is by the contemplation of the ephemeral that God communicates to us the knowledge of Himself. [48]

JILI:
O Thou
Who art absent there,
We have found Thee here.

Thou art nonexistent
As essence,
Existent in Thy person.[49]

The divine obscurity is the nonmanifestation of the Essence; it is logically opposed to the supreme manifestation, which is the unity, so that one cannot attribute to it any quality or name.[50]

PIR VILAYAT: Sufis call this concept *wahdat al-wujud* (the unity of existence). However, some Sufis counter with *wahdat ush-shuhud* (the unity of the witness). If Sufis do not grasp that these concepts are complementary rather than contradictory, they take sides, adopting one or the other. God is not only the object of your cognizance, but the subject — the knower in you.

HAZRAT INAYAT: Truly, the external life is but a shadow of the inner reality.[51] Yes, we recognize God through His traces everywhere. But do not forget that God is beneath all, beyond all, within all, and without all things, the sum total of all that exists and which is knowable — but also what lies beyond man's knowledge.[52] By giving a name to the nameless, by making a concept of someone who is beyond conception, we only make Him limited.[53]

LIGHT

SUBTLE BODY – LIGHT – RESURRECTION

*T*hose signs "on the horizons" of which the Qu'ran speaks, are not simply seen in physical matter, but also in the subtle form of matter.

MURID: What do you mean by subtle form?

PIR VILAYAT: For example the electromagnetic field emanating from our body and the aura of light radiating from our body.

MURID: How do you do it?

PIR VILAYAT: First identify with your subtle body. Then represent to yourself that your body is distilled, thus becoming your subtle body; likewise your subtle body is distilled as your aura.

WORLDS OF LIGHT

The imam of the mosque of Mashhad recites a passage from the Qur'an.

*I*MAM:
God is the light of the heavens and the earth,
He is likened to a niche in which a lamp is burning.
This lamp is in a crystal,
Likened unto a starry pearl,
Which hails from a blessed tree,
An olive tree that is of neither the East nor the West
Whose oil burns without even touching the fire.
It is a light upon a light. (Qur'an 24:35)

A mysterious Sufi carrying the bearing of the Mazdean priest-kings breaks into the gathering. It is Dhu'l-'ulum Azar Kayvan.

Dhu'l-'ulum Azar Kayvan

AZAR KAYVAN:
When I passed in rapid flight
From material bodies,
In every sphere and star,
I beheld a spirit.

PIR VILAYAT: If you meditate at night, observing the starry sky and the galaxies, you will become aware of your relationship with the stars. If you now plunge into this ocean of light you will realize that the light of the cosmos converges as your aura.

MURID: [To Pir Vilayat.] Does this mean that when I meditate, the light I sense surrounding my body, which I call my aura, is the same as the light of the stars?

PIR VILAYAT: Our body does absorb light, whether of the sun and the stars or from the candles or electric bulbs. We reabsorb it into our body cells and radiate it out into the environment. By being aware of this light, you will absorb more. Can you sense the glow all around you?

MURID: I cannot see it, but I do feel something radiant around my body.

PIR VILAYAT: Now try to willfully radiate light as you exhale. Imagine the light hurtling through space at incredible speed. It might even bombard the stars. Exult in the thought that this is the world to which you belong; that you are in exile on earth and that behind the image of your body you are a being of light.

HAZRAT INAYAT: It is in this process that man becomes like a radiant star.[1]

MURID: Even though I sense the glow around my arms and chest, my eyes do not seem to sparkle more than before.

IBN 'ARABI: Remember that light is of two kinds: a light having no rays, and radiant light. As for the light that has no rays, it is the light within, in which self-disclosure occurs.[2]

PIR VILAYAT: To achieve this, one must first turn within and discover the light that emerges from there. We must distinguish between the all-pervading nature of light as we turn within (inhaling) and the radiant light as we reach out (exhaling).

HAZRAT INAYAT: Man's soul is inclined to look outward for its experience, and therefore it remains unaware of the inner being; it turns its back, so to speak, on the inner life, absorbed in the vision of the external through the five senses. The Sufi closes the door through which the soul is accustomed to looking out, and as it finds the doors of its experience closed, a time comes when it turns its back to the external world. It is like changing sides for the soul. The soul then sees before it a different sphere altogether, a sphere that has been within it.[3]

PIR VILAYAT: [Turning toward the murid.] You will have noticed that the inner light does not radiate like a lamp, but is like a web where everything is intermeshed with everything else—like radio waves.

MURID: Indeed, when I turn within, I sense what seems to be a different kind of light than the light I perceive through my eyes.

PIR VILAYAT: When we turn within in our meditation, our consciousness, as it gets inverted, is diffused, and consequently our representation of light has shifted; it is diffused.

SUHRAWARDI: I saw the robe of light altogether in me and I was altogether in it.[4]

HAZRAT INAYAT: Originally the all-pervading light pulled itself together in a center. Then it shot its rays, dividing itself as it proceeded toward manifestation.[5] And by concentrating on that light, you can be instrumental in making this all-pervading light manifest as radiant light. For manifestation, there must be first centralization. From this point manifestation begins.[6] The pure consciousness

Shihab ud-Din Suhrawardi

has... gradually limited itself more and more by entering into the external vehicles, such as the mind and the body, in order to be conscious of the world.[7]

MURID: What practice may develop my ability to manifest as radiant light?

PIR VILAYAT: [To murid.] As you inhale, imagine that you are breathing light through your eyes. The light of the environment is threaded through your optic nerves into your brain. As you hold your breath, imagine it diffusing into the brain cells. Then as you exhale, convert the inner all-pervading light into radiant light converging into a focused beam that radiates through your eyes.

HAZRAT INAYAT: As the sense of sight is situated in the head, it then perceives the light when it is turned within; the brain and the sight, so charged with the light from within, see through life so deeply when turned onto the life without.[8]

PIR VILAYAT: As you cast the inner light (the all-pervading light) forward through your eyes, try to see what transpires through that which appears — for example, try to capture the countenance of a person's face rather than simply observing its apparent features.

[After a pause he addresses the murid.] I can see your eyes are now scintillating!

MURID: Yes, my eyes feel like they sparkle.

MURID: [Upon reflection.] Yes, but I do not know how I got into this state. I was following your instructions blindly. But I want to be able to do it myself.

HAZRAT INAYAT: The key is to awaken dormant faculties in one's body that reciprocate functions in the higher spheres, [functions that] one does not generally use.[9]

MURID: [To Pir Vilayat.] Well then, how does one arouse dormant faculties?

PIR VILAYAT: By training our thinking we create new brain circuits and transform the neurological process as a whole so that it may participate in the new perspectives opening to our awakened consciousness. While providing useful support to our thoughts, our brains in their untrained state limit the outreach of our thinking. However, brain functions can be cultivated to encompass wider dimensions of being.

HAZRAT INAYAT: There is a gradual awakening of matter to become conscious. Through the awakening of matter to increased consciousness, matter becomes fully intelligent in man. Man gains a conviction that frees him from the earth. In matter life unfolds, discovers, and realizes the consciousness that has been buried in it for thousands of years.[10]

MURID: Do you mean that through the mind-body connection one can transmute some of the fabric of one's physical body? Is there a Sufi practice to achieve this?

HAZRAT INAYAT: By the practice of the *dhikr* (remembrance of God), the Sufis arouse certain faculties by quickening the plexi of the autonomic nervous system in which the mind affects the body that otherwise would remain dormant.... We pass to the higher planes of existence in the [elevator] by means of the breath, and hold on to the rope, the physical body, and return to the first floor, the Earth, again.[11]

NAJM UD-DIN KUBRA: The fire of the *dhikr* is visualized as a pure and ardent blaze, animated by a rapid upward movement.[12]

SUHRAWARDI: [To murid.] Do you not see how it is when fire causes iron to become red hot? The iron takes on the appearance of fire — it radiates and ignites.[13]

Shaykh Najm ud-Din Kubra

PIR VILAYAT: Transmute your aura beyond what you commonly understand as physical light just as alchemists transmute lead into gold. Represent to yourself higher frequencies of light: first blue, then mauve, then violet, then ultraviolet. Imagine that this continues beyond the visible range in infinite regress. Do not limit light to what you perceive.

MURID: When I meditate I visualize light. It gives me some sense of what I imagine the heavens to be like. But the light of the heavens cannot be physical. Isn't it another plane?

PIR VILAYAT: In your meditation, try to stalk light beyond your perceptual outreach. Physicists can only ascertain and measure light at the instant it interacts with their instruments in laboratory experiments. Light gives observers no clues as to its behavior before, after, or between measurements. It seems a misnomer to call light matter, even though it is an electromagnetic phenomenon, because unlike any other form of matter it does not have mass.

HAZRAT INAYAT: As man evolves, he ceases to look down upon the earth, but looks to the heavens.[14] If one wants to seek the heavens, one must change the direction of looking.[15] Souls who have become conscious of the angelic spheres hear the calling of those spheres. When the soul is cleared of all earthly shadows, heavenly pictures appear upon the curtain of man's heart.[16]

Rumi responds to the murid's appeal.

RUMI: We are bound for heaven—who has a mind [for] sightseeing? We have been in heaven; we have been friends with the angels. Thither, Sire, let us return, for that is our country. [17]

Shihab ud-Din Suhrawardi,
whose being emanates a radiant light,
adds to Rumi's response.

Shihab ud-Din Suhrawardi

SUHRAWARDI: [With light in his eyes, he draws the attention of the dervishes assembled.] Hail to the company of all who have become mad and drunk with desire for the world of light, with their passionate love for the majesty of the Light of Lights, and who, in their ecstasy, have become like the seven celestial planes.[18]

Then the light of dawn rises on the soul in such a way that that part of the paramount realities emanating from the constellations and the angels, who are their prototypes, predominates in it.[19]

MURID: How do dervishes make the transit from physical light into celestial light?

SUHRAWARDI: When the blazing light lasts long, it obliterates the form — the figures are removed and the individual visitation is effaced.

At that point one understands that what is effaced is giving way to a higher order.[20]

PIR VILAYAT: Suhrawardi is referring to an advanced meditative state in which the Sufi eschews the act of imagination (that is, the representation of forms) and grasps the essence of what appeared as form. At that point she ceases to envision herself as an individual.

BEYOND FORM

*I*BN 'ARABI: Occupy yourself with *dhikr* until the world of imagination is lifted from you and the world of abstract meanings free of matter is revealed to you. Occupy yourself with *dhikr*, remembrance, until the Remembered manifests Himself to you and calling Him to memory is effaced in the actual recollection of Him.[21]

'ATTAR: When the body liberates the soul, the body becomes soul. It is the same body, but luminous.[22] When both your soul and your body become luminous, your body becomes soul and your soul, body.[23]

HAZRAT INAYAT: If you make your soul more subtle in order to turn away from this world, you can find within yourself different worlds by tuning to different planes of consciousness.... You gain a conviction that frees you from earthly conditions.[24]

IBN 'ARABI: The world of the unseen is perceived through the eyes of insight just as the world of the visible is perceived by sight. When these two lights come together, unseen things are unveiled as they are in their essence and as they are in existence.[25]

THE LIGHT OF INTELLIGENCE
The Heavenly Spectator

The voice of Shaykh Najm ud-Din Kubra, who points to the way of illumination in the Sufi tradition, is now heard.

KUBRA: You thought that you were the spectator, the witness of what you experience, but the real witness in you is your angelic counterpart—the witness in the heavens.[26]

SUHRAWARDI: There is a way of looking upon the earth: Rather than perceiving it through the senses, one contemplates its eternal model in one's soul. The scene of the earth triggers off this image which is latent in one. Since these images in one's imagination carry within themselves the hallmark of the angels who project them, and since one's soul is an angel and reflects the archetypal images of the archangels of light and splendor, the forms in the mind will concur with the image that one carries in one's soul.[27]

IBN 'ARABI: Were it not for the celestial light that belongs to the souls, there could be no witnessing, since witnessing occurs only when two lights come together.[28] The object of vision, which is the Real, is light, while that through which the perceiver perceives him is light. Hence light becomes included in light. It is as if it returns to the root from which it became manifest.[29] As long as I am not a light, I cannot perceive anything of this knowledge.[30]

PIR VILAYAT: The secret of realizing oneself as the light of intelligence is to overcome one's conviction that one's consciousness is the witness and to realize that the whole universe is witnessing the cosmos in what we think is *our* act of witness.

INSIGHT VERSUS SIGHT

*P*IR VILAYAT: [To murid.] Ibn 'Arabi and Hazrat Inayat are now drawing our attention to another kind of light. The Sufis call it the light that sees rather than the light that is seen. They also call it the light of intelligence. It conveys meanings, and therefore yields insight instead of sight.

HAZRAT INAYAT: The more deeply we study matter, the more proofs we shall find of intelligence working through the whole process of continual unfoldment…. The dense form of the intelligence… is light. [31] In its finer aspect it is the light of intelligence.[32] Wherever the light of intelligence is thrown, things become clear…. The act of raising the light on high is to hold the torch of intelligence in one's hand in order to see into the external world — that which is seen — and also into the world which is within and unseen.[33] For in all that which is beautiful is intelligence.[34]

PIR VILAYAT: [Addressing the murid again.] You may find that the physical substance of your body, subtle body, and aura is just an infrastructure to sustain an altogether different, nonphysical kind of light, which the Sufis call the *nur-i 'aqli*, the "light of intelligence." The Sufis distinguish between "the light that sees" and the "light that is seen." Now, rather than identifying yourself with your aura, you will identify yourself with the light of intelligence shining on the divine intention, rather than a consciousness picking up information from the existential projections of this intention. You now realize that you are essentially an intelligence that overarches your aura, subtle body, and physical body, which are all infrastructures. This is what is meant by the "light upon a light" in the Qur'an Sharif. Identify with luminous intelligence, and illuminate your eyes with that nonphysical light.

IBN 'ARABI: Self-disclosure also occurs to the nonmanifest dimension of the soul. Then perception occurs through insight in the world of realities and meanings disengaged from substrata…. This only occurs within the meanings.[35]

MURID: How do you grasp the difference between the light that is seen and the light that sees?

IBN 'ARABI: In order to grasp the Image in its absolute reality... it is necessary to have... an organ of vision which is itself a part of the reality of the soul.[36] The symbolic exegesis is creative in which it transmutes things in symbols and causing them to exist at an other level of being.[37] Inasmuch as an object perceived by the senses or conceived by the intellect possesses a meaning, imagination makes of it a symbol which transmutes the simple fact.[38]

'ATTAR: When the body liberates the soul, the body becomes soul. It is the same body, but luminous.[39] When both your soul and your body become luminous, your body becomes soul and your soul, body.[40]

Ghauth ul-A'zam, *Shaykh 'Abд ul-Qaдir Gilani, frail and battered like a lonely tree in the wind, recites as though God were speaking through him:*

For those who cannot stand the brightness of the light of My beauty, I have created the world of shadow, as a protecting veil. And for those who cannot stand the solitude of My oneness, I have created the world of light as a veil.[41]

IBN 'ARABI: Wipe away the phantasmagoria of images and Reality will emerge from inside.[42]

HAZRAT INAYAT: It is [the dervish's] own soul that becomes a torch in his hand; it is his own light that illuminates his path. It is just like throwing a searchlight upon dark corners where one did not see before, and the corners become clear and illuminated anew.[43] It is like throwing light upon problems that one did not understand first; it is like seeing with x-rays persons who were previously a riddle.[44] He sees not only the outside, the surface, but by means of concentration he sees through things as with a torch that illuminates whatever is seen.[45]

Giving vent to his enthusiasm Hazrat Inayat continues:

It is like coming into the same room in the daytime that the soul has once visited in the darkness of the night. Everyone else seems to be open-eyed yet not seeing. It is like when a child is born and begins to see everything new.

MURID: What practice sparks the vision?

HAZRAT INAYAT: Look up first, and when your eyes are once charged with divine light, then you will cast your glance on the world of facts with a much clearer vision, the vision of reality.[46]

The faithful of the Hagia Sophia Mosque in Istanbul are repeating,
"The glances do not reach Him; He reaches the glances."
(Qur'an 6:103)

Pausing for a moment in front of the murids and inquirers,
Hazrat Inayat speaks to them.

HAZRAT INAYAT: The sign of that awakening is that upon every person and upon every object the awakened person throws a light, a light of his soul, and sees that object, that condition, in that light…. He is one whose every glance, wherever it is cast, invites others to reveal to him their secret.[47] Wherever his glance falls, on nature, on characters, he reads their history, he sees their future. Every person he meets, before he has spoken one word to [that person] he begins to communicate with his soul. Before [the awakened one] has asked any question, the soul begins to tell its own history. Every person and every object stand before him as an open book. The willpower works through the glance… and when this light is thrown within one's self, then the self will be revealed; [the awakened person] will become enlightened as to his own nature and his own character.[48]

PIR VILAYAT: Concentrating on this inner light will enable you to discover yourself instead of perceiving the environmental world. Ibn 'Arabi calls this "vision," whereas perception is called "witnessing."

HAZRAT INAYAT: The glance of a sage has the power to open every object and to see through it. In reality it is the light which the sage throws out from within that makes the same things clear to his vision which are only half seen by the ordinary man. Then a person begins to communicate with all things and all beings.[49]

PIR VILAYAT: If you identify with the light of intelligence, you can envision your glance as that of the divine glance, of which it is a focalization; then you will understand the Qur'an. Everywhere you look you will espy the divine countenance trying to transpire through that which appears.

Shabistari, aroused by the discussion, makes a statement that sounds paradoxically cryptic.

SHABISTARI: You are as the reflected eye of the Unseen Person. In that eye, His eye sees His own eye.[50]

IBN 'ARABI: May I contemplate Thee through Thy glance. Through Thine own eyes, may I look at Thy countenance![51]

RUMI: When you look for God, God is in the look in your eyes.[52]

BABA KUHI: [Repeats.] When I looked with God's eyes, only God I saw.[53]

The imam of Karbala recites, "The glances do not reach Him; He reaches the glances." (Qur'an 6:103)

IBN 'ARABI: I see God through the same gaze through which God sees me. Since you do not see Him, He sees you.[54]

[Now prostrating.] Be the one who looks at me and whom I look at, and hide me by thy sight from my sight.[55]

Hajji Bektash

HAJJI BEKTASH:
I was alone with Reality
In His oneness.
He created the world;
Because I formed
The picture of Him,
I was the designer.

MAJRITI THE ALCHEMIST: My image looks at me with my own look. I look at it with its own look.[56]

NAJM UD-DIN KUBRA: You discern nothing whatsoever except by what in you is the like or is a part of it. The precious stone sees only the mine from which it originated; it yearns for that alone. Therefore, when you envision a heaven, an earth, a sun, stars, or a moon, know that this is because the particle in you which comes from that mine has become pure.[57]

IBN 'ARABI: Among these forms (in the celestial spheres) you will recognize your own likeness.[58]

AN ANONYMOUS MANDEAN: I go toward my likeness, and my likeness goes toward me. He embraces me and draws me close as if I had come out of prison.[59]

Majriti

COMMUNICATIONS WITH CELESTIAL HEAVENLY BEINGS

MURID: I do not see how I can recognize a likeness between myself and an angel.

PIR VILAYAT: Consider that by identifying yourself with your body or aura you fail to realize who you are. If you realize that you are caught in one perspective, you can free yourself from that perspective.

HAZRAT INAYAT: The next world is the same as this, and this world is the same as the next. Only that which is veiled from our eyes we call the "unseen" world.[60]

PIR VILAYAT: Our minds translate the abstract into a concrete image of an angel in a perceptual form.

HAZRAT INAYAT: A relation or a friend may appear to a mystic and tell them something about the other side of life....[61] Such a one may see faces never seen before that have once existed in the world....[62] A saint or sage may appear who may guide one further. An angel may appear as Gabriel did to Moses.... As highly evolved a person is, so high is the vision. Sometimes the object of his vision wishes to manifest to him; sometimes he creates the object of his vision before him.[63]

SUHRAWARDI: The experience of authentic rapture in the world of Hurqalya depends on the magnificent prince, Hurakhsh.... There are

Angels praying from *Aja'ibul-Makhlukat* (The Marvels of Creation) by Qasuini, Turkish, probably 16th century.

also visitations and communications from other celestial princes. Sometimes the visitation consists of the manifestation of certain of these celestial princes in epiphanic forms or places appropriate to the moment.... Sometimes the souls of the past induce an awakening or an inner call. Sometimes the apparition takes on a human form....[64] The enraptured see human forms of extreme beauty who speak to them in the most beautiful words.[65]

MURID: How can I distinguish between fantasy and imagination? What reliance can we place on our imagination?

SHABISTARI: Cast aside the vain tales and mystic states and visions. Dream not of lights, of marvels, of miracles. For your miracles are in worshipping the truth. All else is pride and conceit and illusion of existence.[66]

RESURRECTION

*I*BN 'ARABI: Now this journey in God involves the dissolving of the composite nature…. Then the spiritual traveler leaves behind in each world that part of himself that corresponds to it. Let your state be similar to that of the dematerialized spirits of the sublime celestial assembly.[67]

MURID: How can I become like a dematerialized spirit?

SUHRAWARDI: The recluse who has truly realized mystical experience is one whose material body becomes like a tunic which he sometimes casts off…. From that point, he ascends toward the light at will…. This power is conferred by the light of dawn that illuminates his person.[68]

MURID: Leaving behind the body frightens me! It seems like astral projection or a trance state — denying the reality of one's body and by the same token, the physical world.

HAZRAT INAYAT: You need not leave behind your body; you can also become aware of your higher bodies. We are clothed in the garb of an angel, of a jinn, and of a human being. When we see ourselves in the garb of a human being without seeing the other garbs, we believe that we are human beings.[69]

PIR VILAYAT: Simply withdraw your attention from your body identity. Consider it as an ephemeral, evanescent formation made of the fabric of Planet Earth. This identity serves as a support system for who you really are. Envision yourself instead as a continuity in change, not limited to matter.

HAZRAT INAYAT: [Pausing for a minute.] The soul's unfoldment comes from its power, which ends in its loosening the ties of the lower planes. The soul's unveiling is reached by closing your eyes to your limited self... and realizing your immortal self, which is God within.[70]

INQUIRER: But since I live in this limited self, as all people do, what will happen to me if I do truly realize my immortal self?

HAZRAT INAYAT: One is afraid to lose one's self and forgets that it is only the false conception of one's self that one loses.... [71] The soul manifesting as a body has diminished its power considerably, even to the extent that it is not capable of imagining for one moment the great power, life, and light it has in itself. Once the soul realizes itself by becoming independent of the body that surrounds it, then the soul naturally begins to see in itself the being of the spirit.[72] When the realization is no longer in one's imagination but has become a conviction, then one rises above the fear of death. This knowledge is gained fully when an adept is able to detach his soul from his body.[73] Nobody can experience one's eternity from within one's body. Once the soul realizes itself as independent of the body, it is able to touch that part of life in itself that is not subject to death. Man gains a conviction that frees him from the earth.[74]

MURID: I have been trying this unsuccessfully. This is so important for me. Could you suggest a method to apply when meditating to shift my identity that seems perishable to my everlasting identity?

PIR VILAYAT: [To murid.] The secret of awakening from one sphere to another is not only in beginning to identify with one garb rather than another, but in becoming able to transmute the matter of one level of reality to another. It is a method practiced by the Sufis that could be illustrated by the alchemical process of distillation. The secret is to be aware of a process that is already taking place in your body that could be illustrated by what happens to the original chemical compounds in homeopathy: they are transformed into electric charges. This is called ionization: matter has been converted into energy.

MURID: Are you still aware of your body?

PIR VILAYAT: You have to mimic death and imagine that you are resurrecting.

The dervishes at Karbala repeat the Hadith
"Die before death and resurrect now."

HAZRAT INAYAT: By making this body in a different condition you may become conscious of physical annihilation. This could be illustrated by the condition of the body when dying. The body comes to the most material condition. The same condition can be brought about at will. Furthermore, the reaction of everything is quite opposite. If you produce the condition of death at will, in the reaction the opposite will occur. You will experience the resurrection of the body.[75]

IBN 'ARABI: The impossible is imagined as a sensory thing. Moreover it comes into existence in the hereafter as a sensory thing.[76]

Ahsa'i, the Shi'ite esotericist of Iran, who explored the
Islamic view on embodiment and resurrection.

AHSA'I: What returns in reality is matter in a certain form, but this form is precisely the work of the individual person.[77]

PIR VILAYAT: Ahmad Ahsa'i distinguishes four levels of our being:

Ahsa'i

(i) Our physical body (jasad A) which gets dissolved after death.

(ii) Our subtle body, (jasad B) the template of the physical body "that keeps its shape in the tomb irrespective of the disruption of the physical body." It is this subtle body that will serve as an underpinning for the spirit on the day of resurrection.

(iii) Our heavenly correlate (jism A), our particular composition of the celestial light of the heavenly spheres: 'Hurqalya.'

(iv) Our archetypal supra-celestial, everlasting essence which survives death.

At the great moment of resurrection, the supra-celestial essence of our being (jismB), backed by the gist of what we acquired on earth (jasad B) will resurrect. However our celestial counterpart (jasm B) which served as an intermediary between the supra-celestial archetype of our being (jism B) and our subtle body (jasad B) will have fulfilled its task and be reabsorbed in our supra-celestial being.[78]

Jabir ibn Hayyan the Shi'ite alchemist enters the scene.

JABIR: By operating in the retort the same process whereby metals are incubated in the entrails of the earth, we learn the developmental stages of our own transformation. The state of gold is potentially present in gross matter material prima. So it is with our human nature [79]

INQUIRER: [To Jabir.] How do you do this?

JABIR: It is the action of the celestial rush on the terrestrial and subtle bodies jasad and jism that transmutes the terrestrial. We discover this by observing the effect of mercury upon sulphur.

Jabir ibn Hayyan

INQUIRER: What motivated you to make this exploration in nature?

JABIR: I came across an ancient adage attributed to Hermes that suddenly opened infinite perspectives: "As above, so below, as below so above so as to make possible the miracle of a single thing."[80]

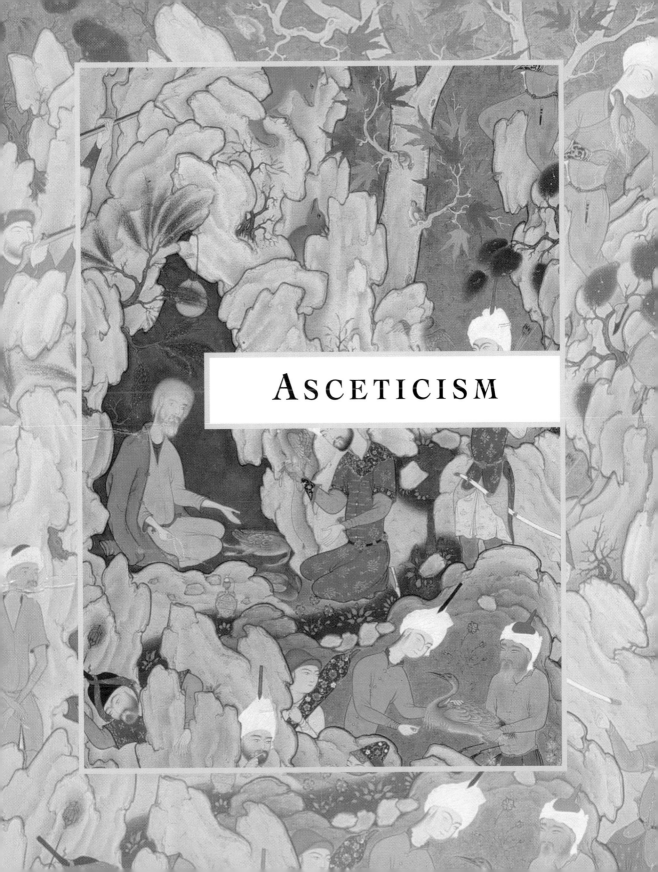

ASCETICISM

Ruined palace in Chitor, India.

THE CHALLENGE

MURID: You speak about God as a hidden treasure and say that He desires to be known, presumably by us. And therefore, you say, He discloses Himself to us.

Now Maulana Jalal ud-Din seems emboldened with imperative derveshi daring.

RUMI: Tear down this house! A hundred thousand new houses can be built from the transparent yellow carnelian buried beneath it, and the only way to get to that is to do the work of demolishing and then digging under the foundations. With that value in hand all the new construction will be done without effort. And anyway, sooner or later this house will fall on its own. The jewel treasure will be uncovered, but it won't be yours then. The buried wealth is your pay for doing the demolition, the pick and shovel work. If you wait and just let it happen, you will bite your hand and say, "I didn't do as I knew I should have."

This is a rented house.
You don't own the deed.
You have a lease,
And you've set up a little shop,
Where you barely make a living
Sewing patches on torn clothing.
Yet only a few feet underneath are two veins, pure red and bright
   gold carnelian.
Quick! Take the pickaxe and pry the foundation.
You've got to quit this seamstress work.
What does the patch-sewing mean, you ask?
Eating and drinking.
The heavy cloak of the body is always getting torn.
You patch it with food
And other restless ego-satisfactions.
Rip up one board from the shop floor and look into the basement.
You'll see two glints in the dirt.[1]

YOU CANNOT BARGAIN WITH GOD

*I*NQUIRER:[To Pir Vilayat.] Rumi has the audacity to ask me to give up all I possess — which I gained by all my hard work — for a phantom of a ghost called God, a figment of imagination, a pure fantasy by which the gullible religious have been brainwashed.

MURID: [Offended by the inquirer's lack of understanding.] Your simplistic mind has missed out on the subtlety of the clues paving the way to the treasure hunt.

PIR VILAYAT: The secret treasure is what we value and pursue in life. What a person values is a gauge of his realization.

MURID: What if there was nothing that I could attain by renunciation? I have struggled so hard to succeed in the world. How can I give up this struggle with no assurance of gain?

PIR VILAYAT: You cannot bargain with God. If you value what you think you might have to give up, don't give it up, because you will find conflict within yourself. The whole of life is a covenant with the unknown. Nothing risked, nothing gained.

The poet Muhammad Shams ud-Din Hafiz, beloved by the Iranians, enters the discussion.

Muhammad Shams ud-Din Hafiz

HAFIZ: God is trying to sell you something, but you don't want to buy. That is what your suffering is — your fantastic haggling, your manic screaming over the price.[2]

RUMI: Look, now here is a bargain: Give one life and receive a hundred…. Go renounce that person in order to contemplate the being of Him. Why, when God's earth is so wide, have you fallen asleep in prison?… Avoid entangled thoughts that you may see the explanation in Paradise. Abandon life and the world that you may behold the life of the world.[3]

An epicurean outsider barges into the gathering.

EPICUREAN: I don't buy all this talk about God and angels and sacrifice. Life is short. Why not enjoy what you can: good food, wine, love, and song?

HAFIZ: You have built with so much care such a great brothel to house all your pleasures.... so you can sneak away from time to time and try to squeeze light into your parched being from a source as fruitful as a dried date pit that even a bird is wise enough to spit out.[4]

[Now he murmurs to himself.] I will have to free myself from every god my mind and this world have ever erected, to free myself from every sterile idol that makes me bow to its lies and wants to strangle my fragile joys and precious winged pen.[5]

RENUNCIATION

*I*NQUIRER: Our civilizations have bequeathed us marvels that enrich us. Are we to give these up for the unknown?

HAZRAT INAYAT: The way of those who renounce is to know all things, to admire all things, to attain all things, but to give all things away, and to think that nothing belongs to them and that they own nothing.[6] So long as you have a longing to obtain any particular object, you cannot go further than that object.[7] Renounce the object you wish to obtain only when you have reached it and have a better one in view.[8]

But do not renounce for gain. What we value, we must seek to attain. But once attained, if you cling to it, the object is greater than you. Rise above it and take a further step in life. You have not really renounced something unless you have risen above it. He who arrives at the state of indifference without experiencing interest in life is incomplete, apt to be tempted by interest at any moment; but he who arrives at the state of indifference by going through interest really attains the blessed state.[9] Renounce the world before it renounces you. All the things one possesses in life, one has attracted to oneself. If you renounce them before that power of attraction is lost, you rise above them.

A group of bedraggled dervishes are repeating a hadith of Prophet Muhammad: "Allah Hu, Allah Hu! Ya 'Azim. Faqri Fakhri (Allah, Allah, O glorious one! Poverty is my pride)."

Ibn Adham, the king who has abandoned his kingdom for the life of the mendicant, confronts the dervishes.

IBN ADHAM: To no purpose you went in for the life of poverty. Since you got it for no price, you do not value it.

A DERVISH: And what price did you pay?

IBN ADHAM: I exchanged the life of poverty for the kingdom of Balkh, and even then I consider that I purchased it cheap![10]

Ibn Adham

MURID: I have a deep longing for freedom, yet I have also become dependent upon things that admittedly I do not need.

HAZRAT INAYAT: All that produces longing in the heart deprives it of its freedom.[11] The real proof of one's progress on the spiritual path can be realized by testing how indifferent one is in every situation in life.[12] Indifference and independence are the two wings that enable the soul to fly.[13] Man seeks freedom and pursues captivity.[14] The moment a person feels that he will no longer remain in prison, the prison bars must break by themselves instantly.

RUMI: Desire only that of which you have no hope; seek only that of which you have no clue.[15] Only when man becomes deprived of outwardly being, like winter, [is there] hope for a new spring to develop in him.[16]

MURID: How can I know when to renounce and when to accomplish?

HAZRAT INAYAT: It depends upon your discrimination: what to renounce and for what; whether to renounce Heaven for the world or the world for Heaven; wealth for honor or honor for wealth; whether to renounce things momentarily precious for everlasting things or everlasting things for things momentarily precious.[17] When man has to choose between his spiritual and his material profit, then he shows whether his treasure is on earth or in heaven.[18] The more closely a person is drawn to heaven, the more the things of the earth lose their color and taste.[19] Verily, who pursueth the world will inherit the world, but the soul that pursueth God will attain in the end the presence of God.[20]

RUMI: [Explaining with a metaphor.] There are thousands of wines that can take over our minds. Don't think all ecstasies are the same. Every object, every being is a jar full of delight. Be a connoisseur and taste with caution. [21]

HAFIZ: [Agreeing.] Learn to recognize the counterfeit coins that may buy you just a moment of pleasure but then drag you for days like a broken man behind a farting camel. [22]

HAZRAT INAYAT: Distinguish need from greed.

ABU TALIB KALIM: Dare you possess without being possessed by what you possess?

PIR VILAYAT: You must assess for yourself what is important for you. You may reach a point where it is more important to fashion your personality as a work of art rather than being opulent, having a luxurious house, and being selfish and unscrupulous.

'Abd ul-Qadir Gilani, "Ghauth ul-A'zam (the Great Reliever)," the austere recluse who inspired Sufis by his holy attunement, adds his voice to the assembly.

'Abd ul-Qadir Gilani

GILANI: You must acquire faith in isolated places, in the desert and the wilderness. Then you may come back to your fellow creatures because then there is work to be done.[23] Then one experiences solitude in the crowd.[24] To prepare His servant for His service, in a first step God alienates him from human beings. Then He causes him to feel at home in the company of savage beasts, wild animals, and the jinn. Once the servant has lost his human loneliness through familiarity with the jinn and the creatures of the wild, God introduces him to the angels....Of all created beings, they are the most beautiful of form and the most pleasant in speech…. Then the servant will go on a journey to every corner of the earth in the company of his guide…. Then things come to him, although he is indifferent to them. It is for his service.[25]

HAZRAT INAYAT: Divine magnetism does not only attract man but both beasts and birds, peris (pixies), houris (fairies), jinns and angels. Even objects are attracted by it. The person [with divine magnetism] becomes the center for all attraction. To this thorough perfection a person can only come by renunciation and annihilation of the individual self.[26]

Ruins at Shar-i-Gholghola in the Nimruz desert, Afghanistan.

BEING OF SERVICE

Murid: I have always assumed that to be of service to people one needs to be engaged with them. But Khwaja Gilani says that God alienates one from other humans.

Pir Vilayat: The moral of it all: Eschew as much as possible pursuing personal gain, which makes one dependent upon circumstances. Rather, involve oneself in the world in order to improve circumstances, unmask injustice, and help those suffering.

The khadims at the Dargah of Khwaja Mu'in ud-Din Chishti at Ajmer, India, are reciting a hadith: "If you cannot serve your friends properly, how can you serve God?"

The imam of Jama' Masjid in Ahmedabad, India, recites an ayah from the Qur'an: "As for those who strive in our cause, we shall guide him to our path." (Qur'an 29:69) *

Mu'in ud-Din Chishti: If you are God-conscious, you will be granted divine power to help those in need.

Inquirer: Some dervishes have reportedly transformed a person's life. This faculty is ascribed to divine power rather than personal power. What is the secret of mobilizing this ubiquitous divine power?

Pir Vilayat: When one awakens one's conscience rather than one's consciousness, then miracles happen. Things come to the one who has committed herself to service when she does not hanker after things. For example, Baba Farid Ganj-i Shakar, a successor in the Chishti Order, was asked to help two people in distress. One was blessed with a miracle, the other was not.

Khwaja Nizam ud-Din Awliya (Mahbub-i ilahi: "Beloved of God"), the successor of Baba Farid in the Chishti line, asks Baba Farid a question.

Mahbub-i ilahi: How is it that after Shams of Sunnam asked for the help of the spiritual power you are invested with by God's grace, since he had insufficient means to look after his aging mother, he got an

Ganj-i Shakar

appointment at the court of the Sultan's son, whereas in the case of the man who begged you to help him in his poverty, nothing happened? Why did you ask Shams to distribute food to the poor and asked the second man to recite a prayer every night?

GANJ-I SHAKAR:
Because in the first case,
Shams needed help to help someone else,

Whereas in the second case,
The man wanted help for himself
And was not prepared to make an effort himself.
The man did not even believe in God
But in my power.
How can someone expect divine assistance
If he does not even believe
In the being
Whose assistance he is calling for?
I do not wield power myself.
I can only inspire people
To get in touch with the Being
Whose providence is evidenced
By the bounty of the universe.[27]

MURID: I find it difficult to keep on concentrating on consciousness. Thinking of some people does indeed inspire me, but some pull me down and arouse irritation in me.

Ibn Sina, also known as Avicenna, (portrait on page 131), the metaphysician who described the stages in the descent from the Divine Mind through the spheres to the human mind, joins the discussion.

IBN SINA: My mentor said, "Abandon those companions who beset you." Every time that you free yourself in order to proceed with zeal, God walks with you.[28] Sometimes, free spirits among men have emigrated toward God.... He makes them aware of the paucity of the advantages of earthly well-being, and when they return to the world, they are replete with mystical gifts. [29]

MURID: Giving up my friends would be a heavy price. I don't like to be judgmental.

ANOTHER MURID: I have a family to provide for and obligations to my fellow beings. Does this mean that because I have obligations to others, I will never be able to experience the divine presence?

HAZRAT INAYAT: The man conscious of his duties and obligations to his friends is more righteous than he who sits alone in solitude.[30] The Sufi chooses a life in the world with renunciation, for he recognizes the face of God everywhere.[31] It is not necessary to become a monk…. Loosen the ties with the physical world…. The Sufi has responsibility for a family, a home, and a profession, business, or trade. But one needs to attach the greatest importance only to what is important in life.

PIR VILAYAT: You will notice, Hazrat Inayat does not tell us to sever the ties but to loosen them. This can be done by loving people but not by being dependent upon their love.

Abu Sa'id ibn Abi'l-Khayr, a gigantic, corpulent, and overbearing dervish, enters the scene. One might have the impression of being in the presence of the emperor of the world.

IBN ABI'L-KHAYR: Sufism is glory in wretchedness, riches in poverty, lordship in servitude, satiety in hunger, clothedness in nakedness, freedom in slavery, sweetness in bitterness, and life in death.[32] The true saint goes in and out among the people, and eats and sleeps with them and buys and sells in the market, and takes part in social intercourse, and never forgets God for a single moment.[33]

Abu Sa'id ibn Abi'l-Khayr

IBN 'ARABI: Renunciation of things can occur only through the ignorance of the one who renounces. His ignorance makes him imagine that the cosmos is far removed from God and that God is far removed from the cosmos. Hence he seeks to flee to God. God gave man an outward dimension and an inward dimension only so that he might be alone with God in his inward dimension and witness Him in his outward dimension after having gazed upon Him in his inner dimension, so that he may discern Him within the midst of the secondary causes.[34]

THE ASCETIC IN THE WORLD

HAZRAT INAYAT: The soul manifests in the world in order that it may experience the different phases of manifestation without losing its way, eventually regaining its original freedom in addition to the experience and knowledge it has gained in the world.

PIR VILAYAT: As they go deeper into contemplation, some dervishes alienate themselves from existential conditions and lose themselves in a primeval, undifferentiated state — something like deep sleep, in the night of time, at the edge of human understanding. From that vantage point, people in ordinary life seem to be caught in total delusion. Very few are able to be God-conscious in life while espying God manifested and existentiated in man.

MURID: So what you are saying is that one does not need to renounce one's life and obligations in the world to find God, but one needs to find an inner independence from circumstances and people while appreciating all the good things of life, loving others, and doing work in dedicated service?

HAZRAT INAYAT: The secret ideal of life and its progress is to become self-sufficient; the key to the secret of democracy is self-sufficiency.[35] What [one] can get from [one's] own self [one] must not look for outside. That is the principal motive of those who are striving for self-attainment. Perfection means self-sufficiency, lack of want. The same is with the mind. By trying to be self-sufficient within oneself, void of all things outside, perfection is attained.[36] One sees a constant striving in… adepts to make themselves independent of outside things as much as possible. On the other hand, worldly people think it progress if they can become daily more dependent on others.[37]

A king becomes a hermit's disciple and takes him valuable gifts. Finally, on offering a brace of ducks, the king realizes that meaningful gifts come from lifelong devotion, the only certain road to heaven. From a 16th century version of *The Haft Aurang* of Jami.

GILANI: When the heart transcends the world, and becomes the guest of the Lord of Truth, it refuses to accept any kind of dependence upon creatures.[38]

MURID: [To Hazrat Inayat.] So you advocate both interest and indifference!

HAZRAT INAYAT: Indifference gives great power; but the whole mani-festation [of creation] is a phenomenon of interest. All this world that man has made, where has it come from? It has come from the power of interest. Creation and all that is in it are the products of the Creator's interest. [39] It is motive that gives man the power to accom-plish things. But at the same time, the power of indifference is a greater one still, because although motive has a power… motive limits power.

MURID: How can one be detached and loving at the same time?

HAZRAT INAYAT: By his indifference [the adept] does not avoid doing all he must for others, only he is independent of the doing of others for himself.[40] Unhappy is he who looks with contempt at the world, who hates human beings and thinks he is superior to them. The one who loves them thinks only that they are going through the same process he has gone through.[41] When he cannot put up with conditions around him, he may think that he is a superior person, but in reality the circumstances are stronger than him.[42] The ego feeds on weak-ness. The ego feels vain when one says, "I cannot bear it." All this feeds the ego and its vanity.

RENOUNCING THE FALSE EGO

ANOTHER MURID: Is there a method in meditation that might help me discover who I am?

PIR VILAYAT: There are steps. First, realize that your self-image is limited by personal bias — it is pure fiction.

HAZRAT INAYAT: The false ego is what does not belong to the real ego, and what that ego has wrongly conceived to be its own being.[43] When that is separated by analyzing life better, then the false ego is annihilated. A person need not die for it. The highest perception of freedom comes when a person has freed himself from the false ego, when he is no longer what he was. All the different kinds of freedom will give momentary sensations of being free, but true freedom is in ourselves. If we identify our ego with all these things that are subject to destruction, death, and decomposition, we think of death as terminal. We identify our soul, which is immortal,… with all that is mortal. Therefore, striving in the spiritual path is breaking away from the false conception that we have made of ourselves, … realizing our true being and becoming conscious of it.

MURID: Just acquiescing that my self-image is a faulty assessment does not free me from it.

PIR VILAYAT: To do this you need to invoke your need for freedom. Since thoughts are sparked by emotions, our indifference can enlist this ability. We need first to deal with our selfishness, which is a feature of our shrunken sense of identity. Reciprocally, our shrunken sense of identity prompts this constriction and defilement of our real selves.

The key is to draw your attention to a deep longing in yourself for freedom and to realize the extent to which your involvement is at the cost of your freedom. From that moment, your self-image will lose its impact on your consciousness, and you can clear of flawed impressions the mirror of your consciousness.

MURID: Many of these dervishes seem to advocate renouncing the world. If I understand well, you are not only balancing detachment with a sense of responsibility in life. You also advocate renouncing the self rather than the world. What does it mean to "renounce the self"?

PIR VILAYAT: As one advances one sees that simply renouncing personal gain is not sufficient, because one's motivations are rooted deeper in the ego.

MURID: Are you saying that to develop divine power I need to give up any satisfaction and reward for my efforts to achieve something worthwhile?

PIR VILAYAT: To renounce the world means renouncing the motivations that a sensitive person eschews in the world— selfishness, greed, avarice, manipulation, dishonesty — with their resulting consequences: unkindness, aggression, cruelty, feuds, war, monstrosity, grossness, vulgarity. To renounce one's self means renouncing one's ego.

MURID: How would you define the ego?

PIR VILAYAT: The ego means "me": the personal, and therefore limited, dimension of one's identity. Each individual's ego customizes the whole universe in a unique way. It could be best defined by its own caricature. The ego becomes bumptious, arrogant, and impertinent the moment one is challenged. These are the very personality features with which one justifies and deceives oneself and others. They make one dependent upon the ego satisfaction that the world offers — concupiscence, ambition for status, callous domination over others, unkindness — leading to a trail of resulting consequences, such as resentment, querulousness, cantankerousness, ruthlessness.

HAZRAT INAYAT: When man in this illusion says "I," in reality it is a false claim.[44] If he feeds [the illusion by] claiming such things he will lose all his power and virtue and greatness.[45] Self-denying [means denying] this little personality that creeps into everything; to efface this false ego which prompts one to feel one's little power in this thing or that thing; to deny the idea of one's own being, the being one knows to be oneself, and to affirm God in that place; to deny self and affirm God.[46]

Annihilation (*fana*) is equivalent to losing the false self, which again culminates in what is called eternal life (*baqa*). [Annihilation] is going through or passing through. Passing through what? Passing through the false conception , which is [necessary in order to arrive] at the true realization…

MURID: Is the ego completely destroyed by annihilation?

HAZRAT INAYAT: The ego itself is never destroyed. It is the one thing that lives, and this is the sign of eternal life. In the knowledge of the ego there is the secret of immortality. You realize your real self by unveiling it from its numberless covers, which make up the false ego.[47]

MURID: Should one annihilate what you call one's "false ego" to find one's real self hidden behind it?

PIR VILAYAT: That false image of ourselves, however inadequate, is the mainstay of our psychological defense system. It gives us resilience against the aggression emanating from the false self-images of others.

Therefore, we need to be careful not to wean our self from our ego prematurely. We must first be able to affirm the authority invested upon us by our identification with whom we are in our cosmic being, which confers divine power.

HAZRAT INAYAT: If you started in life with self-effacement you would never become a self. What would you efface? First you must be a self, a real self that is worth being.[48] Effacing comes afterwards.... Only the illusion is lost; the self is not lost.[49] You need not kill it. Analyze yourself and see: Where does "I" stand? By analyzing life better, then the false ego is annihilated. What is it in us that we call "I"? We say, "This is my body, my mind. These are my thoughts, my feelings, my impressions. This is my position in life." We identify our self with all that concerns us, and the sum total of it all we call "I." You will realize that this conception is false; ["I"] is a false identity. By rising above yourself, this limited self which makes the false ego is broken, and you will rise above the limitations of life on all the planes of existence. Your soul will break all boundaries, and will experience that freedom which is its deepest longing.... It is that realization which brings man to the real understanding of life, and as long as he has not realized his unlimited self he lives a life of limitation, a life of illusion.[50]

MURID: I have always understood that the Sufi term *fana* means the annihilation of the ego.

HAZRAT INAYAT: In man there is a real ego. This ego is divine, but the divine ego is covered by a false ego.[51]

MURID: Can I find my real ego by meditation?

HAZRAT INAYAT: If you dive deep enough into yourself, you will discover your real ego. You will reach a point where you will see that your ego lives an unlimited life.[52] No sooner do we become conscious of our true being and break the fetters of the false ego than we enter into a sphere where our soul begins to realize a much greater expansion of its own being. It finds great inspiration and power, and the knowledge, happiness, and peace that are latent in the spirit.

MURID: You seem to imply that I need to identify with a dimension of myself that is not only deathless but perfect.

HAZRAT INAYAT: The real self can rise to perfection; the false self ends in limitation. The soul, conscious only of its limitation, of its possessions with which it identifies itself, forgets its own being and becomes … the captive of its limitation.[53] Belief in God helps one to annihilate one's false ego.[54] One asks, Can a limited man be conscious of perfection? The answer is that the limited man has limited himself; he is limited because he is conscious of his limitation. It is not his true self which is limited; what is limited is what he holds, not himself.[55] The spirit of limitation is always a hindrance to realizing the spirit of mastery and practicing it. The experience of being powerless is man's ignorance of the power within him.

THE DIVINITY OF THE HUMAN STATUS

ANOTHER MURID: My anger wards off psychological aggressors, keeping them from undermining me and humiliating me, but then I become resentful and aggressive myself!

MURID: I am plagued with compulsive, even obsessive thoughts, emotions, and images that persist. Sometimes I have a feeling that these impressions have become ingrained in me, and that they are irrevocable and adamant. I do not see how I can find God in myself. I am full of flaws, selfishness, and deceit, and I imagine God to be perfect, compassionate, and truthful.

IBN 'ARABI: Do you not see that the Absolute appears in the attributes of contingent beings, and thus gives knowledge about Himself, and that He even appears in the attributes of imperfection and blame?[56]

MURID: I must say, it is a relief to think that those features of my being that I dislike in me (and that others dislike in me as well) are distortions of my real self.

HAZRAT INAYAT: Man does not realize that there is nothing that is not in him. A person who says to himself, "I do not possess that faculty," shows his lack of understanding of what he is.[57] Most men can see only the limitations of human life, and can never probe the heights of their divinity. Comparatively few can do this.[58]

Shaykh Mahmud Shabistari, the popular exponent of intricate Sufi views, speaks up.

SHABISTARI: Behold the world entirely contained in yourself.[59] The world is man and man is a world.[60] Behold the world mingled together: angels with demons, Satan with the archangel, all mingled like unto seed and fruit together and gathered in the point of the present.... The heart of a barley seed equals a hundred harvests.[61] Those to whom unity is revealed see the absolute whole in the parts.[62] Yet each [part] is in despair at its particularization from the whole [63]

Shaykh Mahmud Shabistari

HAZRAT INAYAT: Realize that you have a power in you that is greater than all other powers, and this power is your will. Anger is power, but willpower is greater.[64]

RUMI: Since the Covenant of Alast, both branches — forbearance and anger — have existed to attract men to themselves. Which will overcome, the springs of Paradise or the fires of Hell?[65]

PIR VILAYAT: The fire of resentment can only be extinguished by the light of forgiveness.

A group of Sufi dervishes are reciting a hadith: "Thy light has extinguished my flame."

PIR VILAYAT: When we give way to resentment it arouses the defensive features of our self-image. Our self-image is an incomplete and deceptive notion of ourselves that does not incorporate all the levels of our being. Our identification with our self-image — our false ego — is victimized by unkindness and abuse from the egos of others. If we knew ourselves, the arrows of our abusers fall on the shield of our psychological immunity.

HAZRAT INAYAT: By his forgiveness the power of the mystic can be so great and his insight can be so keen that an ordinary man cannot imagine it.[66] Beyond and above the power of justice is a great power of love and compassion, which is the very being of the mystic.[67]

King Dabshalim and the Sage Bidpai, from a Mughal manuscript, 1610.

RENOUNCE RENUNCIATION OUT OF LOVE

The dapper, elegant and noble poet Farid ud-Din 'Attar intervenes.

'ATTAR:
Renounce the good of the world,
Renounce the good of heaven,
Renounce your highest ideal.
And then renounce your renunciation.[68]

MURID: [Holding her head in her hands ponderously.] Is the noble poet suggesting that I give up my yearning for the heavens? Renouncing my desperate hope of finding refuge in the celestial spheres from the rat race would be a terrible letdown.

RABI'A 'ADAWIYYA: O God! If I worship Thee in fear of Hell, burn me in Hell; and if I worship Thee in hope of Paradise, exclude me from Paradise; but if I worship Thee for Thine own sake, withhold not Thine everlasting beauty.[69]

Farid ud-Din 'Attar

ANOTHER MURID: [Perplexed.] *Murshid*, how could 'Attar have meant that we give up our ideal?

HAZRAT INAYAT: As a soul evolves from stage to stage, it must break the former belief in order to establish the later, and this breaking of the belief is called by Sufis *tark*, which means abandonment. He who fights his nature for his ideal is a saint; he who subjects his ideal to his realization of truth is the master.[70]

PIR VILAYAT: Hazrat Inayat is talking about replacing a simplistic belief with a more enlightened one.

HAZRAT INAYAT: The ideal is a stepping stone toward that attainment which is called liberation.[71] The God ideal is the flower of creation, and the realization of truth is its fragrance....[72] It comes by rising above all that hinders one's faith in truth: the abandoning of the worldly ideal, the abandoning of the heavenly ideal, the abandoning of the divine ideal, and even the abandoning of abandonment. This brings the seer to the shores of the ultimate truth.[73]

MURID: Are you saying that after giving up so much, one no longer needs to? For me renunciation arises out of the indifference of the ascetic; I thought that one's indifference made one overcome resentment.

HAZRAT INAYAT: We are tested in our love. If we judge whether the person is worthy, in that case we limit our love [to trickle through] a channel. But when we allow that feeling of kindness to flow, we have certainly opened that door [through which we must pass] to reach that love which is for God. Human love leads to that ideal of love, which is God alone.[74]

PIR VILAYAT: Renounce worldly pursuits, renounce your false ego; then renounce renunciation out of love.

HAZRAT INAYAT: Those who have accomplished something really worthwhile in the world have had to sacrifice comfort, convenience, pleasure, and merriment. They have had to pay a great price for that attainment; the higher the attainment, the higher the sacrifice it asks. But they value the object [of their accomplishment] higher than the sacrifice; while many renounce the object because they are unwilling to make the sacrifice required.

MURID: What is the difference between renunciation and sacrifice?

HAZRAT INAYAT: Renunciation is made by indifference, sacrifice by love. Deep love on one side, indifference on the other. The mystical indifference is that one retains sympathy and love even at the thought-lessness of a person and expresses it as forgiveness.[75]

BASTAMI

Bastami

UNMASKING THE HOAX

*T*he very thought of the power that will erupt once the false self is annihilated spurs Abu Yazid Bastami's resolve to leave the world to attain awakening. As he experiences the stages of realization, the Sufis at the conference are resonating with him. They accompany him in this deep mystical process, sometimes corroborating his realizations in the light of their own experience, sometimes pointing to the pitfalls on the path, sometimes highlighting apparently contradictory points which, through their dialogues, reveal themselves to be complementary.

BASTAMI: Offer me not what is other than Thee.[1] Grant me the experience of Thy real self in Thy absoluteness beyond existence…. I wish for nothing less than Thy absolute. The bridegroom invited to the divine betrothal does not have to suffice himself with the veil of the bride.[2] God answers, "You are not strong enough to withstand the solitude of My unity." That is precisely what I want.

HAZRAT INAYAT: The mystic goes through different perspectives. When a person awakens to the spirit of unity and sees the oneness behind all things, his point of view becomes different and his attitude changes…[3]

A lone figure walks towards the remains of a citadel at Kandahar, Afghanistan.

The Iranian mystic cries out raucously with even more vehemence in his voice.

BASTAMI: Those effigies I warned you against are not the only furtive effigies, but also all those mirages in which God deceives you in the phantasmagoria of shadows — including the shadows of light.

PIR VILAYAT: By "effigies" Bastami means the way people appear to one's perception — their features or air or deportment.

INQUIRER: What prompted Bastami to affirm that?

BASTAMI: I became a bird whose body was of oneness, and whose wings were of everlastingness. And I went on flying in the atmosphere of relativity for ten years until I entered into an atmosphere a hundred million times as large; and I went on flying until I reached the expanse of eternity, and in it I saw the tree of oneness…. then I looked and I knew that all this was deceit.[4]

HAZRAT INAYAT: Illumination is obtained by rising above one's earthly condition at the command of one's will and realizing one's immortal self, which is God within.

MURID: How can we be mortal and immortal at the same time?

Simurgh flying over a landscape, from the *Khamsah of Nizami*, Mughal manuscrip, 1595.

INQUIRER: Can we stop here and explore what Bastami is saying? He is challenging my mind with concepts of time beyond my understanding.

PIR VILAYAT: Yes, it is indeed challenging to our commonplace way of thinking, but also enriching. By opening our mind to further perspectives, it helps us to make sense of life, which our commonplace thinking cannot encompass. You see, the Sufis make a distinction between the simple process of becoming, called the arrow of time — a condition that may be considered by our ordinary thinking as transient, ephemeral, perishable — and perennity. "Perennity" means continuity in change. This could be illustrated by the fact that the river has a reality although the water that passes under the bridge is never the same, or by the continuity of our body whose cells keep being renewed.

HALLAJ: Thy perennity overarches my transience and my transience is enfolded in Thy perennity.[5] My Lord invested His perennity upon my transience to the point of annihilating my transience in His perennity.[6]

PIR VILAYAT: Another related dimension is evanescence. Evanescence (continual rebirth) recurs over and over again.

That something keeps being reborn does not mean that it continues to live. The Sufis also make a second distinction between perennity and everlastingness. Everlasting means that it will live forever; perennity, however, is continuity in change — the drops of water that flow under the bridge are never the same, but the river they are part of is. The gist of experience updates the programming of the universe.

JAMI: That which is temporal has become everlasting.

PIR VILAYAT: Third, Sufis make a distinction between everlastingness and eternity. In the eternal state there is no change; eternity is invariable. This is what Hazrat Inayat means by our immortality. This is what the Sufis mean by *Azaliyat*.

HAZRAT INAYAT: There is a difference between eternal and everlasting. The word "eternal" can never be attached to the soul, for that which has a birth and a death, a beginning and an end, cannot be eternal though it can be everlasting. It is everlasting according to our conception; it lasts beyond all that we can conceive and comprehend, but when we come to the eternal, that is God alone.[7]

PIR VILAYAT: Fourth, the Sufis make a distinction between the moment of time and the instant. The moment has duration without a definable beginning and end. The instant of time spells a hiatus, a break of continuity. The continuity of the advance of becoming is continually intercepted by something new that cannot be attributed to causality (the effect of the past). An illustration of the instant in time: A pendulum, at the end of its swing, grinds to a halt and reverses direction.

HALLAJ: "Before" does not outstrip Him, "after" does not interrupt Him;... "previous" does not display Him, "after" does not cause Him to pass away.[8]

Data Ganj Bakhsh Hujwiri, the first Sufi teacher to settle in India, responds.

Data Ganj Bakhsh Hujwiri

HUJWIRI: *Waqt* (the instant in time) is that whereby a man becomes independent of the past and the future.... Time cuts the roots of the future and the past, and obliterates concern of yesterday and tomorrow from the heart.... *Waqt* is like a sharp sword that cuts the guilt of the past and the expectations for the future.[9]

MURID: Does Hujwiri mean that we can free ourselves from our guilt?

PIR VILAYAT: Perhaps we will not find absolution but some solace.

MURID: How is that?

PIR VILAYAT: By a pledge. A pledge has a retroactive action upon the past and a deterministic action upon the future.

BASTAMI: During twelve years, I was the blacksmith of my ego, then during five years, the mirror of my heart. And during a further year, I espied that which lay between me and my heart. I discovered a chastity belt that hampered me from outside and it took twelve years to tear it asunder. Then I discovered an internal chastity belt that took me five years to rid myself of. Finally I had a moment of illumination. I considered creation and realized that it had become a corpse; and I performed the burial rites upon it. *La ilaha illa 'llah*, there is none but He.[10]

PIR VILAYAT: [Explaining to the murids.] Bastami is experiencing the state called *al-ama*, the "cloud of unknowing" or "divine obscurity."

A Sufi warming his feet, a 16th century Persian drawing.

JILI: Remember: Unity is the essential, unique manifestation, whereas in the divine obscurity all modes of revelation, while still real, are annihilated under the power of God's essential revelation.[11]

MURID: [To Bastami.] How did you make that shift in your identity?

BASTAMI: I sloughed off my ego as a snake sloughs off its skin.[12]

Medieval cemetery in Assouan, Egypt, 11th–14th century.

IBN 'ARABI: [Turning toward Bastami.] Most of those who seek to know God cease existing, and then cease that ceasing as a condition of attaining the knowledge of God, and that is an error and an oversight. It is not thy existence that ceases but thy ignorance.[13]

PIR VILAYAT: One's existence does not have to cease, but what matters is that the awareness of it does not stand in the way of God-consciousness.

MURID: What do the Sufis mean by the solitude of unity? Unicity — multiplicity! Multiplicity seems to me to be a feature of the world in which I live. So if one says God is alone, then She is not to be found in the world.

JAMI: Do not imagine God as a being segregated from the world. The world in God is God, and God in the world is not other than the world.[14]

HALLAJ: [To Bastami.] By isolating yourself from all existence, and refusing to see God's attributes in man, you do exactly that for which Iblis, the fallen archangel, was condemned.[15] Say "There is no Adam but thee," the one who posited the difference was Iblis.[16]

PIR VILAYAT: [To murid.] You see, Bastami was accused of failing to see God everywhere, just as Iblis was accused of refusing to see God in man. According to the Sufi view, when the mystic shifts the focus of his consciousness from the perspective of the existential word, he experiences a sense of unity. This unity contrasts with the multiplicity of qualities (which Sufis call "attributes") that appear to those immersed in the perspective of the existential world. The mystic thus isolates herself in the solitude of unity.

MURID: What is the difference between unity and unicity?

IBN 'ARABI: The one who is immersed in the vision of multiplicity is in the world in the aspect of the divine attributes. The one who is immersed in the unity is with God in the grasp of God's unity, irrespective of the worlds.[17]

JILI: Every quality is effaced in the unity (*ahadiya*) in which nothing is manifested,[18] whereas unicity (*wahidiyah*) is a revelation of the Essence, which appears as synthesis because of the distinction of God's qualities.

JAMI: The fact that the appearance of the One Being is clothed in attributes does not imply multiplicity in the One Being.[19] The appearance and disappearance of modes of being do not bring about a change in the

An illustration from an Arab manuscript.

absolute realm.[20] When one says that the Real comprises all beings, the meaning is that He comprehends them as a cause, comprehends its consequences, not that He is a whole containing them as His parts.[21]

The theologian Mullah Abu Bakr Muhammad Kalabadhi speaks.

Mullah Abu Bakr Muhammad Kalabadhi

KALABADHI: In a first step, the mystic sees unity in multiplicity. In a next stage, the mystic sees multiplicity in unity.

HALLAJ: [To Bastami.] If one isolates oneself from the world to grasp the solitude of unity, one will be encapsulated in one's own personal self and take it to be God. The one lost in God by the power of love does not isolate himself from the world but is invited by God to participate in the solitude of His unity. Give up isolating yourself from all creation, and then it is God who draws you into His unity.[22]

O THOU! O I!

Bastami falls into a deep silence, measuring all the implications of Hallaj's injunction. It is as though the obstacle in his thinking dissolves and a new horizon opens.

'ATTAR: When the soul has finished its journey to God, the journey in God will begin.[23]

BASTAMI: And He isolated me by means of His own isolation, and unified me through His own unity. He annihilated me from my own existence and showed me His selfhood unhampered by my existence. Then He said to me, "Make thyself one with My oneness, and isolate thyself in My isolation." And I dwelt with Him in His isolation without myself being isolated.[24]

[He pauses as though stymied.]

God said, "I am thine through thee; there is no God but thee."
I said, "Do not beguile me with myself. I am through Thee."
He said, "If thou art through Me, then I am thou, and thou art I."
So I said, "Do not beguile me with Thyself apart from Thyself.
Nay, Thou art Thou. There is no god but Thee."
He said, "O I." And I said, "O Thou." And He said to me, "O thou."
So God's testimony regarding me by Himself concluded.[25]

A Mystic thrown into a furnace from *Nafahat ul-Uns of Jami*, Mughal, 1603.

MURID: Is this what happens to Sufi initiates when they go through the state of *fana?*

The voice of Junayd, the teacher who dismissed his pupil Hallaj for coming to a similar conclusion, rings in the assembly.

JUNAYD: For all trace and idea [of God] that they may experience in themselves, or which through themselves they may witness, has been obliterated from them — they themselves being obliterated in what overwhelms and obliterates them and does away with their attributes. Now God indwells them, though He is far away from them. And although His utter perfection indwells them, He confirms claims against them.[26]

PIR VILAYAT: What Junayd means is that God confirms that people do not recognize these qualities in themselves.

JUNAYD: [Now addressing Bastami.] I am with you in what you are experiencing because I have experienced it myself. He beguiled and deluded me through my own self away from Him. My presence was the cause of my absence from Him; and my delight in contemplation was the perfection of my striving. He bestowed Himself on me; then was I hidden from myself by myself.[27]

HAZRAT INAYAT: When all idea of this external being is gone, then comes the consciousness of the unlimited being of God.[28]

IBN 'ARABI: I request of Thee, O Allah, [that I may fly] toward Thee, and the integration of the totality of my being in Thee, so that my existence will cease to be the veil of my contemplation…. My extinction is in Thee and my permanence is by Thee.[29]

JUNAYD: Then [God] makes the annihilation that is within these souls' annihilation present to them, and shows them the existence that is within their existence.[30]

JAMI: [To Hazrat Inayat.] I find Him when He has made me unconscious of myself…. To be conscious of annihilation is incompatible with annihilation.[31]

Bastami collapses under the impact of the power that is coming through. The murshids in the assembly repeat La ilaha illa'llah hu *silently in respect of what is happening to Bastami.*

MURID: [To Hazrat Inayat.] Can you tell us what is happening?

HAZRAT INAYAT: There is a stage where, by touching a particular phase of existence, one feels raised above the limitations of life and given that power and peace and freedom, the light and life that belong to the source of all beings. In that moment of supreme exaltation, one is not only united with the source of all beings, but dissolved in it, for the source is one's self.

PIR VILAYAT: Having lost sight of his personal identity, the transient pole of his being, he discovered the eternal, unchanging pole.

HAZRAT INAYAT: Annihilation is equivalent to losing the false self, which again culminates in what is called eternal life.[32] The ultimate aim of the eternal consciousness in undertaking a

Hazrat Inayat Khan.

journey to the plane of mortality is to realize its eternal being.[33] Mortality is the lack of the soul's understanding of its own self.[34] The real self is eternal, the false self, mortal. All the attempts made by true sages and seekers after real truth are for the one aim of attaining to everlasting life.

***The faithful at the Shrine of Imam Riza in Mashhad
are reciting, "I breathed into Him from my spirit." (Qur'an 15:29)***

Now Bastami rises to his feet, jubilant.

BASTAMI: Then did He revive me with His life after He had caused me to die. And He said, "I have made thee to live with My life," and I existed through Him. And He said to me, "O Thou." And I said to Him, "O I."[35]

MURID: [To Pir Vilayat.] At first God said to Bastami, "O I." But Bastami was not yet ready to accept it, so God said, "O thou." Why was it only later that Bastami said to God: "O I"?

PIR VILAYAT: God was inviting Bastami into the divine perspective, but Bastami remained caught in his personal perspective and thought of God as "other." When Bastami's personal identity was completely shattered, only then he could see how God saw him as an extension of Himself.

NIFFARI: In the state of union there can be no mediation between God and man, and consequently the dialogue with God is arrested.

HAZRAT INAYAT: The first birth is the birth of man; the second birth is the birth of God. With this new birth, there comes the assurance of everlasting life.[36]

RUMI: [To Bastami.] I am with you in your soul as you are going through this test, to support you in the outcome.

Shushtari, the Andalusian mystic and poet, now speaks.

SHUSHTARI: After extinction I came out, and I eternal now am, though not as I. Yet who am I, O I, but I? [37]

BASTAMI: Through His glance I looked upon my ephemeral condition and it vanished. He annihilated me from my own existence and made me eternal (*baqi*) with His eternity. [38]

PIR VILAYAT: Only after that breakdown can one really become conscious of one's eternity.

BASTAMI: I saw God by God. [39]

PIR VILAYAT: [To murid.] You see, Bastami is experiencing the "further stage" that Ibn 'Arabi had heralded: to grasp God as God is in Himself rather than by means of the clues whereby God reveals Himself.

After the prayers at the Mosque of Bukhara, some Sufis are repeating the hadith an-nawafil: *"When My servant ceases not to draw nigh unto Me by his works of supererogatory piety, I love him. When I love him, I am his sight and his hearing."*

BASTAMI: Thou art my sight in my eye, and my knowledge in my ignorance. Be Thyself Thine own light that Thou mayest be seen by Thyself. There is no God but Thee.[40]

THE INVESTITURE OF QUALITIES

Immersed in his deep process of transformation, Bastami continues to speak.

BASTAMI: My attributes were annihilated in His. And He invested me with His own attributes which none can share. And He called me by His own name.[41]

JUNAYD: Did He not obliterate all trace of me by His own attribute?[42]

IBN 'ARABI: All that one knows of reality is through the qualities — the relations occasioned by the entities of the possible things. If these veils were lifted, unity would erase the existence of the entities of the possible things, and they would cease being described by existence, since they only become qualified by existence through these names. If the names disappeared, the Named One would appear.

PIR VILAYAT: Ibn 'Arabi is referring to the names of God. To manifest the divine nature invested in our being, we must upgrade our idiosyncrasies, the imperfect exemplars of the perfect qualities ascribed to the divine archetypes. The Sufis repeat the names of these qualities — called the Divine Names — to model their personal idiosyncrasies upon their representation of how they could be if perfected.

IBN 'ARABI: Then God makes the adept journey through His names in order to show the adept God's signs within him. The servant comes to know that He is designated by every name. It is through these names that God appears to the servant. Reciprocally, God reveals Himself to Himself in the virtualities of His many names.[43] While we know them only by ourselves.[44]

BASTAMI: My name fell away in His.[45]

IBN 'ARABI: Thou seest thy attributes to be His attributes, and thine essence to be His essence without becoming Him or Him becoming you.[46] We undergo transformations in our states. This transformation manifests as specific influences of those names.

BASTAMI: And I communed with Him in prayer without myself being there. All my own worship was from God, not from me, while I had assumed that it was I who worshipped Him.... I looked upon my Lord with the eye of certainty after He had turned me away from all that was not He and had illumined me with His light. And He showed me marvels from His secret being, and He revealed to me His transcendence. And through His transcendence I looked on my "I-ness," and it vanished away.[47]

And He looked at me
With the eye of munificence,
And strengthened me
With His strength,
And adorned me
And crowned me
With the crown of His generosity.
And He said,
"Glory in My glory
And exult in My exultation
And go forth with My attributes
To My creatures
That I may see My own selfhood
In thy selfhood
So that whosoever sees thee,
Sees Me,
And whosoever seeks thee, seeks Me."[48]

Array me in Your oneness and clothe me with Your selfhood, and bring me to Your unity, so that when Your creatures see me, they will see You. There it will be You, and I will not be there. [49]

HOW GREAT IS MY GLORY!

Now Bastami begins to declare words that shock the orthodoxy.

BASTAMI: *Subhani, ma a'zama sha'ni!* (Glory be to Me, how great is My glory!)

JUNAYD: And when God's manifestations appear to [the Sufis], God causes them to take refuge from Him in their own attributes so that they exult and glory in their isolation.[50]

Shams-i Tabriz, the overbearing, powerful and imperious dervish, cries out, displaying the divine sovereignty coming through his being. Others echo his cries with their own.

SHAMS-I TABRIZ: *Ya 'Aziz!* Glory to Thy magnificence (which I discover within myself)!

IBN ABI'L-KHAYR: *Ya 'Azim!* O God, glory to Thy greatness!

QUTB UD-DIN BAKHTIYAR KAKI: *Ya Qahar!* O God, glory to Thy sovereignty!

BASTAMI: *Ya Wahid, ya Ahad!* Thou art alone in Thy oneness!

HALLAJ: When the instant of vision draws near, the attributes of qualification are annihilated. Then I am severed from my self, and become the pure subject of the verb: No more me, my present I is not me any longer.[51]

He now recalls the perspective that he gained during a meditation where he turned his memory back beyond that of his personal consciousness, seeing things from the divine point of view.

HALLAJ: And God in His perfection turned toward that in Himself that was of the nature of love. It was a ripple within His essence, yet of the very nature of His essence…. And God, the most high, wanted to regard this attribute of desire through aloneness, considering and speaking to it. He turned to pre-eternity, and caused a form to arise that is His form and His essence…. He makes a form arise and in the form are knowledge, power, movement, will, and all of His attributes.[52]

[Now prostrating in deep soul-searching.] Then God elected the human person as the chosen one.[53] *Dhu'l-Jalal wa'l-Ikram!* Thou becomest in man at the end of time the Lord of majesty and splendor! *Ya Malik ul-Mulk!*

Thereupon, God exalted Himself and glorified Himself. He exalted His attributes and glorified His attributes, He exalted His names and glorified His names. Thus He glorified His essence by His essence and glorified each attribute in His essence by His essence….[54] And God saluted this effigy of Himself: man.[55]

Pir Vilayat: Imagine that — having noted something magnificent in your essence, you rejoice in this discovery.

ARISTOCRACY OF THE SOUL, DEMOCRACY OF THE EGO

Murid: The words "Glory be to me" still resonate in my ears. Is that not a clear case of megalomania? Though you say Bastami has lost his personal identity, that does not convince me.

Hazrat Inayat: Where are you to find God if not in the God-consciousness? Yet man, however great, should never claim perfection, for the limitation of his external being limits Him in the eyes of men….[56] When the soul is absorbed in God, one loses the false sense of being and finds the true reality. Then one finally experiences what is termed *baqa-i fana,* where the false ego is annihilated and merged into the true personality, which is really God expressing Himself in some wondrous ways.[57] This is awakening the kingliness of God.

PIR VILAYAT: [To Hazrat Inayat.] All that we have gone through together in this great conference, all that humanity has been moving toward, albeit awkwardly, culminates in your slogan "Make God a reality." But the crux of the question is how to embody the divine power that bursts through when identifying with one's higher self — the divine dimension of one's being — without bloating one's personal ego.

HAZRAT INAYAT: One must honor the aristocracy of one's soul together with the democracy of one's ego.[58] It is the kingly manner, a manner which is known not even to the kings, for it is a manner which only the King of Heaven and Earth knows, a manner that is expressed by the soul who is tuned to God, free from pride and conceit.

MURID: How does one reconcile aristocracy of the soul with democracy of the ego?

HAZRAT INAYAT: Think there is no person lower than yourself while being aware of the kingship within.[59]

MURID: I find it difficult to squeeze the unlimited dimension of my being you call God into the constrictive sense of who I am in real life — and to recognize divinity in people who are offensive.

HAZRAT INAYAT: When the spirit of aristocracy has sufficiently evolved, it becomes democracy. By [gratifying his] ego, man falls from kingship into slavery, and in the end his own life becomes a burden to himself. In order to gain his own kingdom he must destroy the illusion that in satisfying his ego he shows his power; he satisfies only his enemy in satisfying his ego.[60]

> *Bastami's declaration "Glory be to me"*
> *also triggered off an uncomfortable stir among the*
> *participants in the assembly.*

HAFIZ: Do not befool thyself by short sleeves full of patches, for most powerful arms are hidden under them.[61]

MURID: The dervish is reputed to display a demeanor of kingliness. Could you define what that is?

HAZRAT INAYAT: The more I brooded upon this matter, [the more] I questioned whether environment or imagination made a king. The answer came at last: The king is never conscious of his kingship and all its attributes of luxury and might unless his imagination is reflected in them and thus proves his true sovereignty.[62]

MURID: Are you saying that the divine kingship does not rest upon circumstance but upon the king's ability to manifest the divine sovereignty in his being by representing it to himself, thus actuating it in himself?

HAZRAT INAYAT: Yes . . . the kingship of the dervish is independent of all external influences, based purely on his realization and attunement, and strengthened by the forces of his imagination. It is much truer and at once unlimited and everlasting. Verily, [dervishes] are the possessors of the kingdom of God, and all His seen and unseen treasure is in their own possession, since they have lost themselves in Allah and are purified from all illusions. [63]

MURID: So the key to both kingships is the power of imagination?

PIR VILAYAT: In the case of the temporary king, his imagination is sustained by [his] circumstances, whereas in the case of the dervish, his imagination acts creatively upon his being by incorporating the greatness of God into his personality.

MURID: [To Hazrat Inayat .] But I remember you saying that circumstances are what make us believe we are this or that.

HAZRAT INAYAT: If one realizes that power within one and of which one is yet ignorant, that power creates the materialization of its intended object.[64]

The imam of the mosque of Ajmer repeats a hadith:
"God is all power; there is no power but God's."

HAZRAT INAYAT: The willpower in its fullness is divine power; the willpower in its limited state is the individual will.[65]

EMPOWERMENT

The imam at Karbala is reciting, "I am setting on earth a vice-regent." (Qur'an 2:30)

Sahl Tustari, a kingly figure, the erstwhile companion and inspirer of Hallaj, speaks.

TUSTARI: The divine suzerainty seeks a being whose God it is.[66] But this secret of the divine suzerainty has in turn its secret: the secret of the secret of suzerainty.[67]

HAZRAT INAYAT: Divinity resides in humanity. It is also the outcome of humanity. Divinity is to God what the drop is to the ocean. It is of the same nature; but in comparison it is only a drop.

IBN ABI'L-KHAYR: The human being thus became the ambassador of the divine sovereignty.[68]

Sahl Tustari

Kharraz, the incisive metaphysician, comes forth.

KHARRAZ: When God has decided to adopt one of His servants as a companion, He opens to him the door of memory. When the servant exults in this recollection, God opens to him the door of proximity. Then He lifts him to the sphere of respectful familiarity, inviting him to sit on the throne of unicity. At this stage He frees him from the veil and invites him into the sphere of unity, and from this perspective discloses to him the majesty and the magnificence.[69]

IBN 'ARABI: [Overwhelmed by the realization coming through him.] We have given God the power to manifest Himself through us, just as He gave us the power to exist through Him. Thus the role is shared between Him and us.... If He has given us life and existence through His being, I also give Him life by knowing Him in my heart.[70] In discovering His image in me, I recognize Him as being the one of whom I am the image.[71]

PIR VILAYAT: Basically, Ibn 'Arabi postulates four cardinal theorems: By discovering the divine consciousness as the ground of my consciousness as witness, I confer upon God a mode of knowing. By actuating the divine nature that is the ground of my personality, I confer upon God a mode of being. By discovering the divine consciousness as the ground of my consciousness, I confer upon God a mode of being. By actuating the divine nature that is the ground of my personality, I confer upon God a mode of knowing.

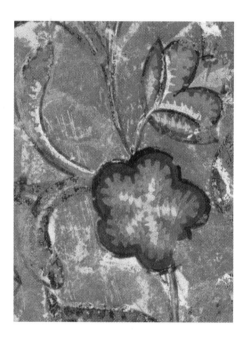

THE SECRET IN YOURSELVES

*I*NQUIRER: Excuse my backtracking. All this high talk about divine attributes, divine essence, divine power is fascinating, but I cannot see how it can be a reality for me. I cannot see God in me. I do not know whom I am. Bastami found it by losing himself in God, but I cannot find God in me.

The Sufis at the mosque of Karbala reflect upon the words of the imam, who is reciting again, "God shows His signs in nature and in the human soul." (Qur'an 51:20-21)*

PIR VILAYAT: You will notice that this *ayah* refers to two kinds of clues: one in the physical environment, and the other in yourself.

MURID: What are these signs in myself?

PIR VILAYAT: Your idiosyncrasies, qualities, potentials. You can only know yourself by earmarking the traces of God's being in your personality.

IBN 'ARABI: All that we know of Him is through ourselves…. Since we know Him by ourselves and from ourselves, we attribute to Him all that we attribute to ourselves.[71] Thus you know Him from your knowledge of yourself.[72]

MURID: I have been looking for God for so long. Do you mean to say that I can find Him through myself?

HAZRAT INAYAT KHAN: There is no way of getting proof of the existence of God except by becoming acquainted with oneself, by experiencing the phenomena that are within oneself.[73] A person asks himself how all he sees affects him and what is his reaction to it all. First, how does his spirit react to the objects or the conditions he encounters, to the sounds he hears, to the words people speak to him? Second, what affect does he have on others' conditions and on individuals when he comes in contact with them?

PIR VILAYAT: Having let go of your deluding self-image, you will turn within; you will be overwhelmed. The whole universe is trying to manifest and fashion itself as you.

HAZRAT INAYAT: One's own self is the object of one's realization. One finds a kind of universe in oneself, and by the study of the self one comes to that spiritual knowledge for which one's soul hungers.[74] If man dived deep enough within himself he would reach a point where his ego lives an unlimited life.

CREATIVITY

THE MIRROR

MURID: I wish to know my real self. I understand that what the Qur'an says is that the qualities and defects of my personality are the manifestations of a deeper reality. If that deeper reality is God, how can it be my real self? I cannot presume like Bastami to be God!

PIR VILAYAT: Remember: We are a condition of God.

MURID: Once more I ask a practical question, not a metaphysical one. How can I know who I really am?

HAZRAT INAYAT: The soul cannot see itself. In order to make the eyes see themselves, one has to make a mirror to see the reflection of the eyes.[1]

MURID: The image of the mirror recurs so often in the Sufi teachings. What does it mean?

IBN 'ARABI: The Real knows Himself, He knows the cosmos from Himself, and He brought the cosmos into existence upon His own form. Hence, it is a mirror within which He sees His own form. [2]

JAMI: From all eternity, the Beloved unveiled His beauty in the solitude of the unseen; He held up the mirror to His own face, He displayed His loveliness to Himself, He was both the spectator and the spectacle.... Although He beheld His attributes and qualities as a perfect whole in His essence, yet He desired that they should be displayed to Him in another mirror, and that each of His eternal attributes should become manifest accordingly in diverse forms. Therefore He created the verdant fields of time and space, and the life-giving garden of the world, that every branch and leaf and fruit might show forth His various perfections.[3]

INQUIRER: Why do the Sufis attach so much importance to the mirror?

PIR VILAYAT: The mirror is a device that provides us with information about ourselves by showing us a projection of our forms outside the spatial location of our bodies. The use of the mirror has triggered a quantum leap in the gradual awakening of intelligence in the human species. One's image is projected as an object instead of being embedded in one's subjectivity — and thereby one gains information about oneself. The mirror objectifies our self-image. By studying this projection of our self-image, we can weaken our identification with it, unmasking the hoax of our perfunctory identity. However, it would be misleading to confine our sense of identity to this projection of our being, which does not encompass our multidimensional identity.

Sufi masters teach us to turn the "mirror of the mind" inward so that impressions from our psychological environment and impressions afflicting the psyche — compulsive thoughts — vanish.

HAZRAT INAYAT: If you find freedom in yourself, you will find that your soul is just like a mirror which shows the object reflected in it instead of its own existence. [4] If you turn the mirror [inward] the reflections are gone. All life's joy and sorrow, ups and downs, are reflected for the time being upon the curtain of the soul, and after the mirror has turned inward, the picture has disappeared. [5]

Place a blind in front of the mirror; consciousness will turn within. To turn within, the Sufi closes the door through which the soul is accustomed to look out, and [once] the soul finds the doors of its experience closed, a time comes when it turns its back to the external world. [6] You will find a kind of universe in yourself.

PIR VILAYAT: You will discover the way that the whole universe is trying to fashion itself in you. Your inadequate self-image stands in the way of your discovering the emergence of the universe in you. When the mirror is turned outward, one not only perceives the physical world but also identifies with one's self-image, whereas when it is turned inward one discovers one's real being. The secret of turning the mirror inward is to downplay the emotional urge that pivots the mirror outward and to highlight one's freedom from one's ego.

MURID: But I want to know who I am. How can indifference — turning my back on the outside world — help me to discover who I am?

PIR VILAYAT: I would call it "detachment" rather than "indifference." It is easier for you to free yourself from your self-image if you realize that it is a faulty realization of who you are. Detachment will help downplay your inadequate self-image, but it needs to be outweighed by enthusiasm in discovering the universe latent in your self.

HOW RELIABLE IS THE MIRROR?

HAZRAT INAYAT: The nature of the soul is transparent, like glass, and when one side of the glass is covered it becomes a mirror. So the soul becomes a mirror in which the outer experiences are reflected when the other side is covered. In order to attain to inner knowledge the Sufi covers the other side of the soul, so that its mirror part may face the spirit instead of the outer world.[7]

IBN 'ARABI: Know that mirrors are diverse in shape and that they modify the object seen by the observer.... Whenever the Real discloses Himself to you, within the mirror of your heart, your mirror will make Him manifest to you in the measure of its constitution and in the form of its shape.[8]

MURID: Are you saying that my perception of what I see as a reflection of my form can be distorted depending on the clarity of my mind?

HAZRAT INAYAT: When the mirror of the mind is distorted, then the image falling upon it is distorted too....[9] Someone who is afraid of you, someone who is against you, someone who is in favor of you, someone who is trying to help you, someone who is thinking of you, someone who is going against your wishes, someone who is standing up for you, all this you can see from a distance if your mind is clear as a mirror. But then if your mind is upset you cannot see it, then what you see is the opposite. Right appears wrong and wrong appears right. Friends turn into enemies and enemies into friends, and everything you see, you see upside down.[10]

PIR VILAYAT: Turn the mirror inward, so instead of reflecting the world it reflects features of your psyche.

SHABISTARI: When one face of the mirror is darkened, the other allows the form to come through. The rays of the sun in the fourth heaven are not reflected without touching the dust of the earth.[11]

MURID: It looks as though there needs to be light and darkness to make a picture. I see! A shift in my perspective allows me to see a different aspect of myself.

ANOTHER MURID: But Hazrat Inayat said that the mirror does not reflect my true being because it is distorted.

HAZRAT INAYAT: If we stand clothed in rags before a mirror, the mirror holds the reflection of our rags, but it is not itself in misery. If we stand covered with pearls and diamonds before the mirror, the reflection of our pearls and diamonds falls upon the mirror, but the mirror does not turn into diamonds or pearls. So is it with the soul. It is neither a sinner nor is it virtuous; it is neither rich nor poor [12]

MURID: Can we clear the mirror of distortion by owning up to our flaws and ploys and thereby get around all the ego games we play?

PIR VILAYAT: One's true being is hidden behind many veils that scramble it into a jumble of superimposed images. The deeper features are distorted by the games of the ego as they transpire through the peripheral layers. But the core is immaculate — the hidden treasure. The only way to see into the depths is to reverse the distortions — purify oneself by the power of authenticity.

Hazrat Babajan

Hazrat Babajan, the brave dervish of Ahmedabad, adds her voice to the discussion.

BABAJAN: Always tell the truth, no matter how much it hurts you or others.[13]

PIR VILAYAT: That is the first step, but it requires digging deeper. By turning inside you may come upon the immaculate core of your being.

'Ali Hamadhani joins in.

HAMADHANI: When the esoteric nature indicated by a man's inclinations and faculties has become pure, he contemplates therein whatever is of the same nature in the macrocosm.[14]

PIR VILAYAT: [Reflecting on Hamadhani's words.] When the impressions from without are dissolved, we find the immaculate form of ourselves. Indeed, our idiosyncrasies can serve as clues leading to the model, the divine archetype, because the archetype is there, inherent within the distortions of the exemplars.

MURID: [To Pir Vilayat.] Does Hamadhani mean that in order to discover one's real self, one must overcome one's defects?

PIR VILAYAT: Of course.

IBN ʿARABI: When your soul has been purified and its mirror has been polished, do not consider the world as it appears in that mirror, but turn your soul toward the dignity of the Essence in its purity, in the perspective of the cognizance that it has of itself.[15]

SHABISTARI: It is in the nonbeing that the secret treasure is to be found.[16]

THE DIVINE TREASURY

*I*NQUIRER: You say God reveals Himself through signs. You say those signs can be seen in the environment and in our nature through forms, and that these forms are clues as to what God is. But how do these forms help us to know God?

The faithful of the Dome of the Rock in Jerusalem ponder upon an ayah *that the imam has recited: "There is no thing whose treasuries are not with us." (Qur'an 15:21)*

*A group of Sufis are reciting,
"God created Adam in His form."*

IBN ʿARABI: Know that there is no form in the lower world without a likeness in the higher world. Between the two worlds there are tenuities that extend from each form to its likeness.[17] God brings us out of the treasuries, that is, from an existence that we do not perceive to an existence that we do perceive. Hence the treasuries contain only the possibilities of things.[18]

MURID: How can one bridge the two levels?

HAZRAT INAYAT: Dive deep within yourself that you may be able to touch the unity of the whole Being.

SUBTLE BODY

HAZRAT INAYAT: When a person is looking in a mirror, his reflection covers the mirror and in that mirror nothing else can be reflected. Therefore, when the consciousness is conscious of anything, it is covered by the thing it is conscious of. The moment that cover is taken away, it is its own self.[19]

PIR VILAYAT: When turning within, we reach a tenuous level of reality where we grasp what seems like a subtle substance permeating matter. Maybe this is the electromagnetic field or even the life field of physics — traditionally referred to as our etheric body. We may have had a sense of having discovered our real countenance, albeit without a profile, fashioned in the fabric of this gossamer etheric body.

It is a wonderful experience: Our physical face appears as a mask through which our real being is trying to transpire. If, turning within, we zoom in on our personal idiosyncrasies, we need to focus deeper.

Shaykh Shihab ud-Din Suhrawardi

Shaykh Shihab ud-Din Suhrawardi emerges from a deep state of contemplation to express his insight.

SUHRAWARDI: These impressions certainly have places in which they appear, as in a mirror, but they are not contained within them; they are bodies in suspension.[20]

HAZRAT INAYAT: The one who turns himself inward, grasping the essence of all things — indeed the essence of the whole Being — is able to enjoy in the seed that fragrance and beauty that delights one in the rose. Likewise, he (so to speak) touches the soul of a thought. Thus things unknown and unseen are known or seen by the mystic. This is called revelation.

MURID: You have been saying that there are indeed clues leading to the secret treasure. I have understood you to be saying that they are of a subtle nature, of our subtle countenance.

PIR VILAYAT: If you could see behind the surface, finding yourself in a transfigured world, you would grasp the template behind that which appears.

HAZRAT INAYAT: It is our mind and our body that draw our soul outward.[21] This space of three dimensions is reflected in the space that is in the inner dimension. The inner dimension is different. It does not belong to the objective world, but what exists in the inner dimension is also reflected in the three-dimensional space.[22]

MURID: I understand from all that has been said that the countenance of the subtle body gives information as to whom I really am.

IBN 'ARABI: Never look at anything without perceiving in it the real face. For the Sufi, nothing appears as a discrete reality, but everything is seen as the face of Reality. [23]

MURID: Does that mean that outwardly I am an inadequate reflection of my inner beauty, and that by contemplating my inner form I can grasp the image of my soul?

PIR VILAYAT: In the depth of your being is your true countenance, the immaculate core. This is what Hazrat Inayat calls "the image of the soul," but its surface is distorted. The outer forms mask the inner form, causing distortion. Should you turn the mirror deeper inward, the previous reflections are erased and you will discover the hidden countenance behind your face.

[He pauses, pensively.] Perhaps the most amazing feature of the mirror is that it projects not just the countenance behind one's face, or the true nature behind one's personality, as the object of one's self-knowledge. The mirror even projects one's eyes, which reveal the subject in one rather than one's personality.

MURID: To turn the mirror inward, do you have to change the focus of your consciousness so that it is no longer focalized in the personal vantage point?

PIR VILAYAT: When you turn within, your consciousness will shift into a very different mode, in which everything is interspersed with everything else.

HAZRAT INAYAT: All things and beings on the surface seem separate, beneath the surface they approach nearer to one another, and in the innermost plane they all become one. This plane of three dimensions is reflected in the space that is in the inner dimension; and what exists in the inner dimension is also reflected in the three-dimensional space.

PIR VILAYAT: You will discover yourself to be like gossamer. If you shift your identity further inward, you will discover yourself as a being of light. The reflection in a mirror is an ephemeral construct of light modeled by the features of the light of the environment — its light is continually feeding from the environment and diffusing into the environment, eventually into outer space. Moreover, it changes as the environment changes. The like is to be found if you become aware of yourself. Your aura is an ephemeral, evanescent construct that reflects your psyche. You will discover that the way that latent idiosyncrasies of your personality erupt as formations in this fabric of light provides you with information about yourself.

PHOTOGRAPHIC PLATE

*M*URID: I still feel that the metaphor of the mirror can be incomplete and misleading. Turning the mirror away by the non-emotion of indifference seems like denying something stirring in the depth of my unconscious, something that I must deal with.

> *The faithful of Ribat Tit-n-Fitrr, Morocco,*
> *pick up the conversation, citing the hadith:*
> *"La rahbaniya fi'l-islam*
> *(No monasticism in Islam)."*

HAZRAT INAYAT: [To Pir Vilayat.] One needs to distinguish between a mirror and a photographic plate. Memory can be limited to a photographic plate — the impression memory takes remains there, and when a person wishes to recollect something, this faculty helps him. As soon as he wants to recall an experience, he puts his hand, so to speak, on the particular plate that has received the impression experienced. No experience received from sight, or smell, or hearing, or touch, or taste is lost.

ANOTHER MURID: [To both Hazrat Inayat and Pir Vilayat.] I really need clarification. This is all so confusing! On one hand, you say impressions can be erased by turning the mirror away from what is reflected. On the other hand, you say that impressions can really be imprinted on one's psyche.

HAZRAT INAYAT: We are endowed with the same faculty as that of a mirror — that of being able to erase impressions — and also that of a photographic plate that retains impressions.[24]

PIR VILAYAT: The mirror in us can diffuse impressions by turning away, and the photographic plate in us can reconstruct images. Both metaphors are true. The way of the ascetic is to turn away from the world by that non-emotion one might call indifference, detachment, or independence. This certainly gives one a kind of inscrutable power that one finds in the recluse. Asceticism also works as an anesthetic against psychological pain. But by turning away one is not owning up to real emotions that remain covered and are not dealt with. These emotions may erupt dramatically at any time. Hazrat Inayat offers a more realistic metaphor, the photographic plate, because it does not discard impressions.

HAZRAT INAYAT: No. It is still different. A soul not only takes an impression like a photographic plate, but it becomes nurtured by it.[25] A reflection on a photographic plate remains, but does not live; the reflection upon the mind lives, and therefore it is creative.[26]

PIR VILAYAT: The metaphor that Hazrat Inayat Khan is proposing goes beyond the photographic plate. It is that of a seed that, nurtured by the earth, the water, the air, and the sun, transforms all these into a plant. Therefore, unlike a mirror, input is not reflected away but reconstructed. The metaphor of the photographic plate is an apt illustration of the operation of creative imagination. The picture can be dismantled and reformed again by the creative power of imagination —our faculty of imagining.

HAZRAT INAYAT: Imagination becomes a ladder on the path of the mystic. Besides, if it were not for imagination there would have been no art, there would have been no literature, there would have been no music; these are all outcomes of imagination. Imagination can create beauty of much higher and greater value when it is directed inward.[27] Naturally, the mystic begins his work with the ladder of imagination, and actual experience follows.[28]

THE CREATIVE POWER OF IMAGINATION

KHWAJA ABU HASHIM MADANI: The soul draws its power from the divine source. The soul tuned to God becomes as beautiful as God and begins to express God through all it does, expressing in life the divine manner. The one who has this power is entrusted with the secret of life. The contemplation of divine power discloses before his view the mighty hand of God working through all things and beings. [29]

PIR VILAYAT: [To the murid who spoke before.] If circumstances can have such an impact on our imagination, think how strong the impact is when imagination configures an attribute in our personality!

MURID: Do you really mean that if I think I am strong, it will make me strong?

PIR VILAYAT: Yes, but…

An inquirer interrupts, intrigued by the idea.

INQUIRER: This sounds very exciting. I am an actor, and when I play a role, if I really believe I am that person the public believes it, too.

MURID: [To Pir Vilayat.] But do you find that thinking you are strong has a lasting effect and makes you stronger in real life?

PIR VILAYAT: It is exciting that our built-in imagination allows us to fashion our subtle bodies and unfurl the qualities of our personalities. Just imagine that instead of confining yourself to your self-image, you carry the psychological genes of the whole universe in you; only your self-image constrains you from acknowledging who you are in the cosmic dimension of your being.

HAZRAT INAYAT: Think that the same power that moves the stars and the sap in the trees is in you. By man's limitations he… buries the divine creative power in his mind.[30] The experience of being powerless is [man's] ignorance of the power within him.[31] The soul has in it a potentiality, a creative power as its divine heritage. On the one side man is limited and imperfect, on the other side he represents the unlimited and perfect.[32] The difference between divine and human will is like the difference between the trunk of a tree and its branches; and as from the boughs other branches and twigs spring, so the will of one powerful individual has branches going through the will of other individuals. By contemplating upon divine attributes man awakens the same attributes within himself.[33]

RECREATING THE SELF

HAZRAT INAYAT: As the whole of nature is made by God, so the nature of each individual is made by himself.[34] Other arts cannot be compared with the art of personality. In a real artist a distinct personality is developed that expresses itself in everything he does. The artist becomes art itself, and whatever he does becomes a beautiful picture. The character is not born with man's birth, the character is built after coming here.

PIR VILAYAT: We have within us a creative power not confined to creating works of art or situations. It has the ability to fashion our personality as well.

HAZRAT INAYAT: In the making of personality it is God who completes His divine art. With the personality of man, man can only take a human point of view, whereas with the personality of God man has to take God's point of view.

INQUIRER: Tell me how!

PIR VILAYAT: You may fashion your personality as a sculptor fashions a statue.

MURID: This is precisely what I would like to do, but how should I proceed?

PIR VILAYAT: The key is imagination.

MURID: Is there not a danger that what we take for imagination is wishful thinking?

PIR VILAYAT: One needs to distinguish between fantasy and creative imagination.

MURID: How can one distinguish the two?

PIR VILAYAT: Random thoughts erupting facetiously lack coherence. They are the products of the human mind when disconnected from its cosmic seedbed. You could exchange them for something completely different and you would not know the difference. If one were to change one note of a classical piece of music, a good musician would immediately spot the mistake. That is because the structure of a genuine work of art rests upon an orderliness on a macrocosmic scale. If you remain encapsulated in your self-image, constricted by your personal biases, your imagination runs amok in fantasy. Instead, you need to link the idiosyncrasies of your personality with the cosmic attributes of your real being. The fashioning of your personality is intrinsically linked with the whole formative process of the universe. Therefore the Sufis stalk the secret of creativity: Creativity is being able to reverse our consciousness and to imagine God dynamic rather than static, to become what She is — becoming by and in us.

DISCOVER YOUR BEAUTY

*I*NQUIRER: Do the Sufis practice watching their image, seeing it in its entirety without identifying with it?

PIR VILAYAT: Yes. For the Sufis, this ability replicates on the human scale what is happening on the cosmic scale: God, acquiring a further knowledge of Himself by projecting Himself into a form that conveys clues as to God's real being beyond form.

HAZRAT INAYAT: In the external *dhikr* [you fix before you your] own form, with open eyes. You are able to produce your image before yourself. First, move your right hand toward your left shoulder and then to your right shoulder, making a horizontal line. Then raise the hand upward to the center of the forehead, and then draw it downward in a perpendicular line. This makes it a cross. As you draw the horizontal line, say, "This is not my body." Now draw your hand downward and say, "But this is the temple of God."

IBN 'ARABI: God is the mirror in which thou seest thyself as thou art — His mirror in which He sees Himself.[35]

JAMI: O Thou whose picture confers splendor to the mirror, nobody has ever seen a mirror without Thy portrait. No, no, because, thanks to Thy grace, in all mirrors it is Thou who appeareth, not Thy portrait.[36]

'Ala' ud-Daulah Simnani

'Ala' ud-Daulah Simnani, whose teaching is entirely founded upon the experience of the encounter with light, speaks out.

SIMNANI: I am the mirror of Thy face; through Thine own eyes I look upon Thy countenance.[37]

MURID: How could our physical form give clues as to the beauty of God?

HAFIZ: If you could borrow my eyes, you would realize how beautiful you are.

RUMI: By God, when you behold your own beauty in the mirror you will be the idol of yourself.[38]

MURID: This sounds so heartening, but my face is full of flaws and I am afraid they register my disgruntled nature.

PIR VILAYAT: Imagine a flawed copy of a perfect model, which is distorted in our form through our defilement.

RUMI: And if you see an ugly face in the mirror 'tis you; and if you see Jesus and Mary, 'tis you…. He puts your image before you.[39]

JILI: Know that when active imagination configures a form in thought, this configuration is created. Since the Creator exists in every creation, this figure exists in you. Thus the imaginative operation concerning God must be yours, but simultaneously God exists in it.[40]

Jili

IBN 'ARABI: Imagination causes archetypal notions to descend into perceptible forms.[41]

HAZRAT INAYAT: Once a person has an imagination, a thought, it exists. In what form does it exist? In the form the mind gives it. As the soul takes a form in the physical world, a form borrowed from the world, so the thought takes a form which is borrowed from the world of mind.[42]

MURID: But I thought that God was beyond form!

IBN 'ARABI: The Necessary Being whose pure essence is incompatible with all form is nevertheless manifested in a form. [43] When meanings are embodied and become manifest in shapes and measures they assume forms, since witnessing takes place through sight.[44]

HAZRAT INAYAT: The mind is a magic shell in which a design is made by the imagination, and the same imagination is materialized on the surface.[45] On the physical plane this process may be seen in a more concrete form.[46]

The voice of Ahsa'i is heard.

AHSA'I: What returns in reality is matter in a certain form, but this form is precisely the work of the individual person.[47]

HAZRAT INAYAT: Consciousness awakens in matter, where it was... buried for thousands of years.

Zib un-Nisa, the renowned though hidden Mughal princess, exclaims:

The mirror of my heart I burnish bright
Until, reflected fair for my delight,
The self's eternal beauty greets my sight.[48]

If thou thinkest of the rose,
Thou wilt become the rose.
If thou thinkest of the nightingale,
Thou wilt become the nightingale.
Thou art a drop,
And the Divine Being is the whole.
Whilst thou art alive,
Hold the thought of the whole before thee,
    and thou wilt be the whole. [49]

Zib un-Nisa

Khwaja Nizam ud-Din Awliya

Khwaja Nizam ud-Din Awliya, the successor in the silsilah
*(chain of the transmission) of the Chishti Sufis, whose tomb is in the
precinct of Delhi that bears his name, joins in.*

AWLIYA:
Where's the mind to grasp Your sovereignty?
Where's the soul to mirror Your majesty?
Beauty's face
I know You could unveil,
but where are eyes to behold Your beauty?[50]

THE POET, KHUSRAU:
Through Nizam ud-Din Ilahi's
Existence
The world is kept alive.
In the same manner,
All forms are kept alive
By the Spirit.

RUMI

Rumi

THE ECSTASY OF LOVE

*R*UMI: Today the king came secretly before the madmen, and their spiritually possessed souls began to lament.[1]

As if from nowhere, Shams-i Tabriz bolts in with sunshine on his face and a stentorian voice. He is dressed in an odd mixture of red and black stripes of cloth sewed on a gunnysack held together by ropes, and wears numberless rings, necklaces, and amulets of doubtful value.

SHAMS-I TABRIZ:
The man of God is a king 'neath a darvish-cloak.
The man of God is a treasure in a ruin.[2]

[He pauses for a moment.]
This is love: to fly heavenward,
To rend, every instant,
A hundred veils.
The first moment, to renounce life;
The last step, to fare without feet…[3]

Shams-i Tabriz

RUMI: Suddenly I asked, "Who is that king?"

"Shams ud-Din, the king of Tabriz," and my blood began to boil.[4] His image passed by and the spirit said, "That is he, the king of the cities of No-Place."[5]

INQUIRER: [To Rumi.] That is a singular concept: a king without territory! But the impression you give is that Shams-i Tabriz has made a powerful impact on your being.

RUMI: How should you know what kind of king is my inward companion!… When Shams-i Tabriz becomes our guest, we are multiplied hundreds of millions of times!… In my love for Shams of Tabriz, I am a sultan wearing a crown — but when he comes to the throne, I am his vizier.[6]

MURID: How could that be, since he said he is a ruin?

RUMI: Wherever there is a ruin, there is hope for a treasure — why do you not seek the treasure of God in the wasted heart?[7]

[Looking at Shams.] An ever-renewed radiance comes to me from Thy beauty and comeliness.... I have seen my beauty in Thy beauty. I have become a mirror for Thy image alone.[8] [Rumi is overcome with tears.] Everything I was, thought, or said was Him. If not for the Beloved, what is there in the world? The Beloved is all, the lover just a veil.[9]

Detail of a Qur'an, Surat un-Nisa, "Woman" (IV, 121), copied in Iraq or Persia, probably late 10th century.

BEAUTY AND MAJESTY

Hazrat Inayat: There comes a time in one's evolution when every touch of beauty moves the heart to tears; it is at that time that the Beloved of Heavens is brought to earth.

Rumi: Constantly Thy image is before my eyes![10]

Murid: [To Pir Vilayat.] I try to perceive Shams through Maulana Rumi's eyes.

Rumi: I have never seen a face like this! [To Shams.] How dost thou resemble that form that I heard talk about?[11]

The Mevlevi dervishes in Konya are reciting a hadith of the Prophet: "I saw my Lord in the most beautiful of forms."

Inquirer: This intensity of love disturbs me; it seems so personal! It seems to be infatuation for a beautiful face.

RUMI: Do you know what shines into the heart's mirror? Only he who knows purity knows the image displayed there.[12] Show not Shams-i Tabriz's coin to him who has not our fineness.[13] When love provides replenishment upon replenishment, the spirit gains deliverance from this dark and narrow body.[14] How long will you look at the form of the world's body? Return, and behold its inward mysteries![15]

INQUIRER: What disturbs me more, Rumi is extolling his love for another man's beauty.

PIR VILAYAT: Do not mistake sublime friendship for love between the sexes.

RUMI: She (woman) is the radiance of God.[16] Made attractive to men is the love of desires — women.[17]

MURID: But Maulana eulogizes the beauty of Shams's face!

> *Echoes are heard from the Sufis at the tomb of*
> *Baba Kuhi in Iran, who are reciting a* **hadith:**
> *"Everything perishes except the face of God."*

PIR VILAYAT: The Sufis are always speaking metaphorically. They are not referring to our commonplace perception of the physical world, but are referring to "that which transpires from behind that which appears," which is evanescent. This explains why the Sufis make a distinction between the form and the image.

HAZRAT INAYAT: To love the formless in a form requires self-abnegation.

RUMI: [Prostrating.] In order that we might remember each other, I gave my wounded heart to Thee and took Thy image.[18]

NIZAM UD-DIN AWLIYA: Only that one whose love distracts and destroys me can heal me.[19]

RUMI: The beauty of the unseen form is beyond description; borrow a thousand illuminated eyes.[20] Since His image is so, behold how His beauty must be! His beauty displays itself in the image, which cannot display Him.[21] If you remain in forms, you are an idol-worshipper.[22] Let the Unseen Form come and remove you from form.... Pass beyond the form and behold the meaning![23]

[Looking into Shams's eyes.] Pride of Tabriz! Sun of God and the religion! Tell me: Are not all these words of mine Thy voice?[24]

PIR VILAYAT: [To the murid.] The Sufis make a distinction between *tasawwur-i murshid* — the picture, even the image of one's teacher — and *tawajjuh,* shifting one's consciousness into that of the teacher, then the Prophet, then God.

MURID: [To Rumi.] What do you mean by the "Unseen Form"?

RUMI: It cannot be seen because the spirit cannot bear to see Thy face unveiled.[25] When the spirit was annihilated in contemplation it said, "None but God has contemplated God's beauty!"[26] [Pensively.] The universe displays the beauty of Thy comeliness! The goal is Thy beauty.[27]

MURID: I am not clear now if Rumi is talking about Shams's beauty or the beauty of God.

PIR VILAYAT: It is God's beauty manifesting through Shams that so intoxicates Rumi. But I must add: for the Sufi dervishes: the purpose of life finds its ultimate expression in God's beauty. You may have noticed that at first Maulana Jalal ud-Din said the motive beyond existence was love; now he is saying it is the beauty manifesting in a human form.

RUMI: God said to love, "If not for thy beauty, how should I pay attention to the mirror of existence?"[28]

INQUIRER: But infatuation in a person is still idolatry, even if it is toward the image of the ineffable countenance behind his face, Why do the Sufis not seek the absolute as do the yogis in *samadhi*?

HAZRAT INAYAT: Love could not manifest unless there were an object to love.[29] The Sufis explain it thus: that God, the Lover, wanted to know His own nature; and that therefore through manifestation the beloved was created, in order that love might manifest.[30] All that seems good and beautiful one can imagine in its perfection as far as one's imagination reaches, calling it the beauty of God; for beauty is only manifest to our view in its limitation. It is in God alone that we see beauty in its perfection. There is no object of which we can say that it is perfectly beautiful, nor is there anyone except in our ideal to whom we can attribute all beauty.[31]

PIR VILAYAT: [To murid.] You see, for the Sufis, the mystic's love for God is a response to God's love for humanity, and love for another human being is a stepping stone toward divine love. Actually, we are really searching for our self in the loved one, only to find that the divine Beloved disclosing Herself by manifesting and actuating Herself in the loved one helps us find our real self.

RUMI: Were ought to be contemplated other than the everlasting Beloved, how would that be love? That would be idle infatuation.[32]

IBN 'ARABI: It is He who in every beloved being is manifested to the gaze of every lover.[33]

JAMI: Every beauty manifested in beings is an expression of His perfect beauty, from which it derives.[34] Without the mirror that I am, the beauty of Thy beloved being would not appear. The Lover is God and so is the Beloved.[35]

HAZRAT INAYAT: What we see of our Beloved before our physical eyes is the beauty that is before us. That part of our Beloved which is not manifest to our eyes is that inner form of beauty of which our Beloved speaks to us. In order to see this beauty, one must develop spiritually so that this beauty may manifest to one's view.[36]

PIR VILAYAT: You see, to seek God manifesting as man, the dervishes try to get into the divine consciousness and thus experience a sublime emotion that they call divine emotion. It is ecstasy, an uncanny state of inebriation.

RUMI: At this moment I am so drunk in thee.[37] The king Shams-i Tabriz has placed the cup of intoxication before me.[38] O Saki of the Sufis! Give us a wine that does not come from vat or grapes.[39] Hark, O heart! Be not deceived by every intoxication!... A single drop of heaven's wine will tear your spirit away from all these wines.... Know that every sensual desire is like wine and hashish — it veils the intelligence and stupefies rationality.... Know that in this world, the drunkenness of sensuality is despicable compared to the angel's intoxication.... Take this other wine, not that red or amber one. This one will make you the master of meaning and deliver you from outward forms.[40]

Moved by Jalal ud-Din Rumi's and Shams-i Tabriz's love,
the dervishes start whirling, the stardust of their bodies like planets
in the galaxies.

RUMI: [Exulting in ecstasy.] We came whirling out of nothingness scattering stars like dust. The stars made a circle and in the middle we dance. Turning and turning it sunders all attachment. Every atom turns bewildered... and it is only God circling Himself.

Dancing Dervishes, Timurid Period, Iranian, School of Herat, Diwan, 1490.

INTOXICATION

R UMI: You still find it difficult to grasp the shaykh's state.[41] Perhaps Shams-i Tabriz will intoxicate you from beyond the two worlds and remove you from yourself.[42]

MURID: I find the life we have created in our civilization so boring! This is precisely what I am looking for. I am looking for ecstasy. This is why I sought initiation.

PIR VILAYAT: The Sufis disclose to us and incite in us a very special emotion. Not to be confused with what one normally calls love, it is ecstasy, love transmuted into something nobler, touching upon the sacred. Ecstasy is aroused in the dervishes as they espy all that lies in wait in the universe called God: majesty, beauty, compassion, sovereignty — all the imaginable attributes made human so that the dervishes are able to discover those divine attributes in themselves. This attunement shatters, transfuses, overwhelms, and transfigures one's whole being.

HAZRAT INAYAT: I remember my *murshid* said, "There are many forms of friendship. But the friendship formed in the search of truth, in the love of God, is greater than any other in the world."[43] To love God, the murid learns by the friendship of murshid. He begins to feel in murshid something of the fragrance of that flower, which is the love of God.[44]

IBN 'ARABI ADDS: For the image to lead to the divine model it needs to be transmuted by the lover — and moreover, he is transfigured thereby.[46]

The faithful of Tashkent are reciting, "Wherever you look is the face of God." (Qur'an 2:115)

MURID: How do the Sufis gain ecstasy by discovering the divine face in every face?

PIR VILAYAT: By trying to see things from the divine point of view. In his or her search for the divine model, the Sufi values the countenance behind the face as the device whereby God discovers Her splendor manifesting as beauty and majesty in the mirror of the existential world. By the same token, that which transpires through that which appears serves as a clue whereby God discloses Her beauty and majesty to us, as a spur to enhance our love for God.

SHABISTARI: One day at dawn the fair one entered my door and woke me from my sleep of slothful ignorance. The secret chamber of my soul was illumined by His face, and my being was revealed to me in its true light.... He said, "This self-seeking of thine is a hoax keeping thee back from Me. To glance at Me for a moment is worth a thousand years of devotion."[46]

Rabi'a 'Adawiyya, the Sufi saint, enters the scene once again.
The veil that conceals her face espouses its
contours, revealing the beauty that speaks of a being in love.
All are moved by her presence.

RABI'A 'ADAWIYYA: [Oblivious of the gathering.] I have loved Thee with two loves, a selfish love and a love that is worthy of Thee. As for the love which is selfish, I occupy myself therein with remembrance of Thee to the exclusion of all others; as for that which is worthy of Thee, therein Thou raisest the veil that I may see Thee.[47]

TRANSCEND

COMPLEMENTARITY

*P*IR VILAYAT: [Asking Ibn 'Arabi.] I remember your saying when you conversed with Abu Yazid Bastami that the ephemeral gives clues to the eternal. Could the reciprocal not also be true? If you include the antipodal point of view — the divine point of view — in your individual point of view, is it by the contemplation of the eternal that we make sense of the ephemeral?

IBN 'ARABI: Yes, indeed there is a further stage. God said, "When you have entered into My paradise, you have entered into yourself (into your soul) and you know yourself with another knowledge different from that which you had when you knew your Lord by the knowledge you had of yourself."[1]

PIR VILAYAT: Now you know yourself through the knowledge that God has of Himself through you.

NIFFARI: God said, "When thou perceivest thou seest limitation openly, and thou seest Me at the back of the unseen. When thou art with Me thou seest the opposite."[2]

IBN 'ARABI: The ephemeral is not conceivable as such, that is, in its ephemeral and relative nature, except in relation to a principle from which it derives its possibility, so that it has no being in itself, but derives it from another to whom it is tied by its dependence.[3] For man is incapable of appropriating the divine knowledge which is applied to those archetypes in their state of nonexistence.... However, the Essence only reveals itself in the form of the disposition of the individual who receives this revelation.[4]

HAZRAT INAYAT: It is not self-knowledge that leads to divine knowledge but divine knowledge that leads to self-knowledge.

MURID: [Responding to Pir Vilayat.] I am getting lost in all this rhetoric. I assume that what you mean by the ephemeral is that life is passing by. How can I maintain a consciousness of the eternal when I live in the ephemeral?

PIR VILAYAT: God in Her eternity discovers Herself in our ephemeral nature. Therefore, while the ephemeral gives clues to the archetypal — that is, the eternal — the archetypal gives us clues to understand the ephemeral. The Sufi, rather than trying to grasp God through his own nature, is responsive to the act whereby God reveals Herself.

Kharraz, gifted with incisive philosophical insight, makes a declaration.

Kharraz

KHARRAZ: God can only be known by the synthesis of antinomic affirmations.[5]

MURID: What does "antinomic" mean?

PIR VILAYAT: It refers to complementarity. Complementarity means that there are two poles of the same reality.

HAZRAT INAYAT: The same reality can look different according to the vantage point from which you look at it. There are two awakenings: man awakening in the divine perspective and God awakening in the human perspective.

MURID: Excuse my asking again the same question I have asked many times before. I want to know my real self. I have come to understand that my being has two complementary dimensions, personal and transpersonal. I also understand that the transpersonal is coextensive with all beings, and that it is what most beings call God. But knowing the theory does not give me experience. When identifying with my personal self I try to grasp my higher self, but it evades me.

PIR VILAYAT: That is the wrong method. You must arouse your higher self and identify with it rather than try to grasp it, and it will reveal itself. You must give up using your will to pull yourself upward. Consequently, you will be receptive to the divine action upon you — the action of the universe upon each fragment of itself — pulling you up into rarified regions of your being, from one sphere to the next.

IBN 'ARABI: God acquaints travelers through the spheres with what corresponds to them in each world by passing with them through the different worlds.[6]

HAZRAT INAYAT: Truly perfect realization can be gained only by passing through all the stages between man (the manifestation) and God (the only Being), knowing and realizing ourselves from the lowest to the highest point of existence, and so accomplishing the heavenly journey.[7]

PIR VILAYAT: This is precisely what is meant by awakening: downplaying one's identity at the personal level, and highlighting each of the higher levels of one's being one by one, identifying with these higher bodies.

IBN 'ARABI: In contemplating [God], we contemplate ourselves, and in contemplating us, He contemplates Himself.[8] The contemplator is simultaneously the contemplated. There is no other than He, nor is there anything that emanates from Him other than Him. Thus is man at once ephemeral and eternal.[9] Consider therefore this reciprocal dependence of ideal realities and individual realities.[10]

MURID: [To Pir Vilayat.] This seems to be a contradiction, since Ibn 'Arabi just said that it is by Himself that He knows Himself.

PIR VILAYAT: God discovers Himself by disclosing Himself to you and you discover Him by reciprocating, by predicating qualities in your personality that you generally ascribe to yourself. God's qualities are the archetypes of which your qualities are the exemplars. The image in which God reveals Himself to Himself — and by the same token, to you — is the image through which He manifests Himself.

NIFFARI: God said, "When thou seest Me, how shalt thou say to that which appeared, 'Where is His secret?' or to that which was hidden, 'Where is His disclosing?'"[11]

IBN 'ARABI: [To Niffari.] He knows Himself and we know Him not.[12]

JILI: This cannot be known by reason, nor conceived by insight. Only he who has attained divine intuition savors the pure taste of the total revelation that one calls the "divine unveiling"; and it is the object of the perplexity of the perfect among the initiated.[13]

HUJWIRI: Knowledge of God is attained by unceasing bewilderment of reason. It cannot be acquired but is miraculously revealed to men's hearts.[14]

HAZRAT INAYAT: The mystic touches the reason of reason, the cause behind the cause, the purpose beyond the purpose.

JILI: It is the consternation of the intelligences.[15]

IBN 'ARABI: So there is nothing but perplexity upon perplexity.[16]

HAZRAT INAYAT: Be not surprised if God Himself is perplexed!

A FURTHER UNVEILING

Ibn 'Arabi comes forth with the next step.

IBN 'ARABI: Then comes another unveiling, through which our forms in God will become manifest to you.[17]

MURID: My form in God! What could that mean?

PIR VILAYAT: Ibn 'Arabi has just announced the next step: It is through Him that you know yourself." [To murid.] Instead of identifying with your form, try to envision that your form is the means by which God is revealing Herself to you in a tangible way, just as an archetype reveals itself through its exemplar. By identifying ourselves with the personal dimension of our being, we fail to realize the bounty of our potential and ascribe this to God, who we imagine as "other." If you think of God as other, then you can envision that the archetypes of our form are only present in God. If you consider that all is God, then of course our forms are Her own. It is through your form and the features of your personality that God is known to you.

IBN 'ARABI: He never manifests Himself to His creatures except within a form, and His forms are diverse in each disclosure. [18] God imagines the forms that reveal Him to Himself.[19]

DOES GOD GAIN KNOWLEDGE OF HIMSELF THROUGH YOU?

Ibn 'Arabi comes bursting forth with a further realization, looking at things with the force of insight of one who has gained the key to the secret treasure. Now he announces the decisive breakthrough — the next step.

IBN 'ARABI: The knowledge you may glean by grasping in yourself the divine archetype of which you are an exemplar is only the first degree of a Sufi; the second is knowing oneself through the knowledge that God has of Himself through you.[20]

HAZRAT INAYAT: The purpose of the whole creation is the realization that God Himself gains by discovering His own perfection through His manifestation.

PIR VILAYAT: [To murid.] You will remember the *hadith* "Whosoever knows himself has access to the knowledge of God."

A scene in a mosque.

That was the first stage in spiritual development. The second stage is the reverse: inferring the archetype of your idiosyncrasies as their divine model, which enables you to discover yourself. Now the third step consists in trying to look at your idiosyncrasies and at the world as contemplated from the divine vantage point. Imagine God discovering Herself in the form in which She discloses Herself to you — your own form.

IBN 'ARABI: God created perception in you only that therein He might become the object of His perception.[21]

HAZRAT INAYAT: Intelligence becomes known to itself when there is something intelligible. Therefore, the knower had to manifest himself, thus becoming an object to be known.

MURID: But how can I discover myself through the knowledge that God has of Himself through me?

PIR VILAYAT: In your meditation, think that you are so much an intrinsic part of the universe that your thoughts are the way the universe thinks through you.

HAZRAT INAYAT: The experience of every soul becomes the experience of the Divine Mind. Not knowing that God experiences this life through us, one is seeking for Him somewhere else.

NIFFARI: God said, "He is not Mine who sees Me and himself through his own making to see; he only is Mine who sees Me and himself through *My* making him to see."[22]

IBN 'ARABI: The cosmos is nothing other than [God's] self-disclosure within the forms of the immutable entities, which cannot possibly exist without that self-disclosure.[23] God's knowledge of the things is His knowledge of Himself.[24]

Illustration from the *Maqamat* of Hariri, painted by Yahya ibn Mahmud Wasiti, from Baghdad, Iraq, 1237.

PIR VILAYAT: By immutable entities, Ibn 'Arabi means the divine code. The universe, having actuated its potentialities as the cosmos homonized (embodied) as us, discovers itself only inasmuch as we discover the universe in and as ourselves. Thus God discovers Herself by revealing Herself to us in our own image in the measure that we espy in ourselves the divine archetype, of which we are the exemplar. This requires us to shift our consciousness to the antipodal standpoint and try to see things from the divine point of view.

GOD INDEPENDENT OF THE WORLD

MURID: [To Ibn 'Arabi.] Do you mean that God gains further knowledge of Himself through the way I manifest His being in my own? Do you mean that God needs us to know Him? Do you think that my participation in this creative imaginative process could be of benefit to the divine self-discovery? I always understood that God was independent of the world.

The dervishes at the tomb of Shaykh 'Ali Sabir
at Kalyar are reciting,
"God is independent of the worlds." (Qur'an 3:97)

IBN 'ARABI: [Pauses to listen, then explains.] In respect of Himself, He is "Independent of the worlds," but in respect of the most beautiful names (attributes) of God, which demand the cosmos because of its possibility in order for their effects to become manifest within it, He demands the existence of the cosmos.[25] By clothing Himself with His modes of being He discloses Himself to Himself.[26] For that cause God brought me into existence.[27]

Since the Essence is independent of the world, He is independent in the absolute sense. He has no needs, and there is nothing that His creatures can contribute to Him that He has not in Himself. He nurtures the possibility of existing. What He created was for you.[28] The one who enjoys this independence and has manifested the world did not manifest it by necessity. He created beings so that they may enjoy existence in order to free them from the solitude of the void, to give them the possibility of acquiring the divine attributes, and to make them His vice-regents. All of this was done by dint of altruism, because He chose not to remain the only holder of those things that He gave.[29]

A medical consultation, illustration from *The Book of Kalila and Dimna*, Persian School, 14th Century.

There is a chilled silence, then signs of protests in the assembly at the audacity of the presumption that man could confer anything upon God.

Now Hallaj comes forth with a determination in his gait and conviction in his gaze, and points his finger at Ibn 'Arabi. He speaks with the resonance of divine wrath in his voice.

HALLAJ: Shall the eternal be known through the diurnal?[30] How can contingent creatures who have alienated themselves from Him by the abyss of time try to prove the Creator by His works?[31]

[Moved by the power of this thought, he kneels in prayer.] Henceforth there is no longer, between me and God, an intermediary explanation, neither proof nor miracles can serve now to convince me! … The proof is His, by Him, toward Him, in Him — it is the very attestation of the true: a knowledge that explains itself…. Such is my existence, my evidence, and my conviction, such is the divine unification of my *tawhid* and of my faith!… Those whom He isolates in

Abu Zayd with a half-naked old man who speaks to him in verse, illustration from Hariri's *Maqamat*, Baghdad, 13th century.

Himself, whom He endows with gifts of wisdom, in secret and in public — such is the consummation of existence of those to whom He gives ecstasy, sons by blood relation, my companions, my friends![32]

MURID: [Whispering to Pir Vilayat.] I don't understand what Hallaj is implying.

PIR VILAYAT: Mansur Hallaj questions how the human consciousness that has alienated itself from the source of consciousness could know that source. He considers our human knowledge of God's thinking just an inference, infinitesimal in comparison with God's knowledge of Himself beyond creation. How, then, could this knowledge add anything to the knowledge that God has of Himself? By the same token, his statement further implies that the eternal cannot be known through the ephemeral, which is precisely what Shaykh Ibn 'Arabi has been saying. I remember my father saying, "It is not self-knowledge that leads to divine knowledge, but it is divine knowledge that leads to self-knowledge."

JAMI: The real Being is one, but He possesses different degrees[33]

HALLAJ: He holds Himself apart from the states of His creation. In Him there is no mingling with His creation....[34] To describe Him, there are no attributes.[35]

JILI: All these changes or evolutions in forms... in all that is relation or connection [within the existential cosmos] arise only from the modes according to which God reveals Himself to us, while He remains in Himself eternally just as He was before He manifested Himself to us.[36]

MURID: [To Pir Vilayat.] I cannot yet see the difference between what Hallaj and Ibn 'Arabi are saying.

PIR VILAYAT: You see, they agree that God is trying to reveal Herself, Her thoughts, Her intention, to us. For Ibn 'Arabi, God uses the creatures who are an extension of Her to actualize all that is potential within Her being. We are not "other than God"; God knows Herself through Herself as us. For Hallaj, however, there is an abyss between God and us creatures.

[After a pause.] To understand this concept more clearly, we need to distinguish between the knowledge that God has in the principle of His being, irrespective of the existential state, and the knowledge that God gains when these principles of His being (that is, the archetypes of the divine planning) are applied existentially by the fragmentation of Himself in nature. There is a difference between knowing God whose eternal being is the model of what we find on earth, and discovering what becomes of the eternal archetype as it unfolds in existence. It depends on what side of the veil separating the existential state from the transcendent state you are looking from.

MURID: In the course of this stupendous dialogue, we have moved breathtakingly from one stage of discovery to another, from one perspective to another. I have lost a sense of the developmental stages in the realization of the Sufi mystic.

PIR VILAYAT: Remember, the Sufis are in search of the secret treasure commonly called God. This treasure paradoxically loves to be known yet conceals itself under the very veil that manifests itself to protect us from its power. We are told that God reveals Herself through clues in the existential world and in our own psyches. These manifest as forms, images, or idiosyncrasies — character traits. God imagines the forms that reveal Her through our own creative imaginations. By homonizing (embodying) Herself as us, She gains through diversification a further perspective, a mode of being other than that which God is in Her transcendent, ineffable state.

Ibn ʿArabi now advances.

IBN ʿARABI: According to a *hadith* that is sound on the basis of unveiling, but not by way of transmission, God said something like this: "I was a treasure but was not known, so I loved to be known and I created the creatures and made Myself known to them. Then they came to know Me." So God [knows] Himself through witnessing in the manifest. But He knows that He could not be known in His transcendence — in the respect that He knows Himself in the principle of His being.[37]

Ibn Sina

That which is revealed is not the world. Consequently, the knowledge of ourselves through the divine perspective, insofar as its form appears to one as a form in God, is by necessity limited by our ability to grasp it through ourselves. The perspective of unity is lost.[38]

IBN SINA:
His knowledge
Is not a consequence
Of the things known
. . . .
For His knowledge of things
Is the reason for their having being. [39]

BEYOND IMAGINATION

Now Ibn 'Arabi pauses as though focusing upon the lifting of the ultimate veil, what is perhaps his ultimate realization.

*I*BN 'ARABI: And yet there is a further stage. At an advanced stage one learns to grasp God as He is in Himself rather than the knowledge gleaned of Him.[40] Then thou understandest that thou knowest God by God, not by thyself.[41]

HALLAJ: [God] penetrates in [the awakened], takes them by surprise, overcomes them, touches upon them, and blinds them when passing through them.[42]

PIR VILAYAT: [To murid.] You will notice that at first Ibn 'Arabi said, "In respect of His relationship of independence, He knows Himself and we know

Abu Zayd and Harith, illustration from Hariri's *Maqamat*, Egypt, 1337.

Him not." And now suddenly he has a flash of insight that brings him closer to Hallaj. What Hallaj is saying is that, although we creatures are removed from God by "the abyss of time," sometimes God discloses to those He chooses His knowledge of Himself. Sometimes He stoops down from His pinnacle in a flash and gives you a burst of ineffable realization. The differences between Hallaj and Ibn 'Arabi do not represent differences in doctrine, but differences of perspective according to the developmental stage of the mystic. Ibn 'Arabi announces this further stage as the next step after proceeding through the previous stages. Remember, we have been saying that God can only be known through clues. Now Ibn 'Arabi is announcing a whole quantum leap: The stage of God beyond His manifestation in the existential world is revealed to the mystic who has eschewed identifying himself as the witness.

MURID: [To Pir Vilayat.] Shaykh Ibn 'Arabi is contradicting himself. He first said that God cannot be known in His transcendence and then he says that one can grasp God as He is in the principle of His being.

PIR VILAYAT: In our ordinary state of consciousness, we have no idea of the being of God except through clues, through form. We take the clues to be the reality they reveal. The great shaykh announces, however, a more advanced stage at which God's intention behind manifestation can be espied. God unveils His being, beyond form, bereft of the veils that reveal Him.

IBN 'ARABI: [Continuing in the same state of consciousness.] Make [God] prevail in accordance with what He is in Himself rather than with the knowledge that you have of Him.[43]

NIFFARI: God said, "The least of the sciences of My nearness is that you should see in everything the effects of beholding Me, and that this vision should prevail over you more than your gnosis of Me."[44]

A sermon in the mosque, *Maqamat* of Hariri, probably Syrian, 1222–3.

THE KNOWN RATHER THAN
THE KNOWLEDGE

Now Ibn 'Arabi's eyes sparkle at the breakthrough of his insight.

IBN 'ARABI: One may see the Real behind the veil of things.[45] Unveiling conveys knowledge of the Real in the things. Things are like curtains over the Real. When they are lifted, unveiling takes place. The Real is not known in the things without the manifestation of the things and the lifting of their properties. The eyes of the common people fall upon the properties of the things, but the eyes of those who have the opening of unveiling fall only upon the Real in the things. Among them is he who sees the Real in the things, and among them is he who sees the things while the Real is within them. Between these two there is a difference. When opening occurs, the eye of the first falls upon the Real and he sees Him in the things, but the eye of the second falls upon the things, and then he sees the Real within them because of the existence of the opening. If you witness creation, you will not see the Real, and if you witness the Real, you will not see creation. So you will never see both the Real and creation at the same time: You will witness this in that and that in this, since the one is a wrapper and the other enwrapped.[46] When that veil is lifted disclosure takes place. The veil may become transparent. [47]

MURID: How do I acquire the knowledge that Ibn ʿArabi is announcing, opening myself to God's disclosure of Himself, eschewing any clues in the world or in myself?

IBN ʿARABI: At this stage, one must avoid looking for one's instructions in the realm of imagination… which only gives indirect indications regarding pure archetypes.[48]

PIR VILAYAT: [To murid.] You will notice that clues are displayed in forms. Now we are reaching beyond form. We pick up signals or clues by acts of consciousness. Consciousness is the awareness of an object. God, however, cannot be the object. To grasp that reality we call God, we need to eschew the act of consciousness. Then intelligence, which is the ground of consciousness, will take over.

HAZRAT INAYAT: Intelligence confined to knowledge of phenomena becomes limited, but when it is free from all knowledge, then it experiences its own essence. Consciousness must always be conscious of something. When consciousness is not conscious of anything it is pure intelligence. Consciousness means the loaded intelligence, intelligence charged with knowledge, with impressions carrying ideas. It is intelligence when there is nothing before it to be conscious of. When there is something intelligible before it the same intelligence becomes consciousness.

IBN ʿARABI: Knowledge is a veil upon the known.[49]

NIFFARI: God said, "The knower tells of his knowledge, the gnostic tells of his gnosis, the mystic tells of Me…. Knowledge is My veil, gnosis is My speech, mysticism is My presence."[50]

PIR VILAYAT: Why seek for the known when you can know the Knower?

STALKING THE UNATTAINABLE

*H*AZRAT INAYAT: There is a time in life when a passion is awakened in the soul which gives the soul a longing for the unattainable,[51] and if the soul does not take that direction, then it certainly misses something in life for which it is innately longing and in which lies its ultimate satisfaction. This craving for the attainment of the unattainable gives the soul a longing to reach life's utmost heights.

PIR VILAYAT: The reason for that word "unattainable" is because it leads us always further — we can never claim to have reached it.

MURID: [To Hazrat Inayat.] What do you mean by "awakening"?

PIR VILAYAT: Awakening is downplaying the commonplace perspective and highlighting another perspective, which surfaces when seeing from a loftier dimension of one's being — and by the same token, from the universe.

MURID: [To Hazrat Inayat.] How do you feel when awakened?

HAZRAT INAYAT: Consciousness has become so light and so liberated and free that it can raise itself and dive and touch the depth of one's being. [52] Every atom, every object, every condition and every living being has a time of awakening.... Sometimes there is a gradual awakening, and sometimes there is a sudden awakening.[53] There is an awakening from childhood to youth, then to a mature age. One's point of view, one's outlook in life is changing.[54] There comes a time when all that one had acted in one's mind, all that one had believed, appears quite the contrary to what it seemed before. Things that people take to heart will seem of little importance, and he finds that all his life he has given his thoughts to something which does not last, which does not even exist. When one's soul is awakened, one becomes in one moment a different person. To some persons it comes in a moment's time — by a blow, by a disappointment, or because their heart has broken through something that happened suddenly. Sometimes after one has made a mistake, by the loss that mistake has caused, the outlook becomes quite different.[55] There is a time when the wind blows and brings good tidings as if it awakens from sleep; then the waves rise. All this shows struggle. It shows that something has touched it and made it uneasy, restless. This makes it yearn for release, liberation from ignorance.

MURID: [To Hazrat Inayat.] How is higher consciousness attained?

HAZRAT INAYAT: By closing our eyes to our limited self, and opening our hearts to the Perfect Being who is formed in our heart.

MURID: [To Pir Vilayat.] Pir Vilayat, is there not an intermediary level between what you call the existential state and the no-man's-land of the unattainable? I am longing to discover the memory of the higher levels of my being that I have lost touch with in my daily life.

IBN 'ARABI: As for the Sufis, they have spiritual journeys in the intermediate world during which they directly witness spiritual realities that are embodied in forms that have become sensible for the imagination. These sensible realities convey knowledge of the spiritual realities contained within these forms. Thus the ascensions of the saints are the ascensions of their spirits triggering off the visions of their hearts, whereby they perceive forms in the intermediary world and of embodied spiritual realities.[56]

MURID: [To Hazrat Inayat.] Can a person living on Earth really grasp something of the conditions in the higher spheres?

HAZRAT INAYAT: True exaltation of the spirit resides in that it has come to Earth and has realized there its spiritual being.[57]

ON THE JOURNEY

*P*IR VILAYAT: Trying to retract memory further and further back prior to one's birth will act as a catalyst, triggering off one's awareness that at the higher levels of one's being one is still living and functioning in those spheres.

MURID: Can I actually remember my condition prior to my conception?

HAZRAT INAYAT: We live in the world to which we are awakened, and to the world to which we are not awakened we are asleep…. The soul in its manifestation on earth is not at all disconnected from the higher spheres. It lives in all spheres, though it is generally conscious only on one plane.[58]

MURID: How does one awaken one's higher self? This is exactly what I am yearning for. What are the steps?

PIR VILAYAT: As we have already seen, first you must shift from identifying yourself with your physical body and start identifying with your subtle body. To start with, draw your attention toward the zone around your body, particularly your upper arms. It feels fluid, even volatile, rather like gossamer. It is like a magnetic field. Then as we have already learned, sense the light around your body; identify with it, then shift your identity from one level of light to the next. Rather than casting your glance on the physical world to gain insight, turns your glance onto these ascending planes, the first being the celestial spheres.

IBN 'ARABI: What [God] first discloses to you is His gift of command over the material order…. It is the unveiling of the sensory world which is hidden from you.[59]

MURID: How does one shift from one plane to another?

PIR VILAYAT: Having recognized the features of your ancestral inheritance, can you envision yourself as having existed prior to your having inherited these features from your ancestors?

HAZRAT INAYAT: One's grade of evolution depends upon the pitch one has attained; it is a certain pitch that makes one conscious of a certain phase of life. There is a stage at which, by touching a particular phase of existence, one feels raised above the limitations of life. At that moment of supreme exaltation. One is not only united with the source of all being but dissolved in it, for one discovers that that source is one's very self.[60] It is just like touching the presence of God. Awakening in life is as if one were awake in the middle of the night among hundreds and thousands of people who are fast asleep.[61] When one awakens to the spirit of unity, one sees the oneness of all things. One experiences everything as the self of one's being. One sees the divine evidence in every face, as one might see the painter in the painting.[62]

Hallaj

Hulegu Khan's astronomers in the observatory at Maragha, miniature from a manuscript of the *Nusrat Namah* in Turkish, Bukhara, 16th century.

DIVINE COMMUNION

Hallaj seems to be impelled by an imperceptible and ineffable presence.

HALLAJ:
Here I am, O my secret, O my trust;
Here I am, O my aim, O my very significance!
  I call Thee; no,
It was Thee who beckoned upon me.
How could I have deemed to say, "It is Thou" if
  Thou hadst not already whispered, "It is Me"?
O end and aim of my destiny!
O my very language, my stammering![1]

Hallaj

There is a superlative "I" behind my "I" forever;
O take away my "I" that so ails me from between
Thou and me.[2]

IBN 'ARABI: My God, how much I call Thee, and yet it is
Thee who calls![3]

HALLAJ: [Prostrating, oblivious of all around.] *Subhan Allah. Subhan Allah!* Thou art there as the tears between my eyelids, or the blood within the cockles of my heart.[4] Thy image in my eyes, Thy recollection on my lips, Thy abode in my heart.[5] [He kneels in prayer, in the grip of *hal* (ecstasy).]

[Repeating.] *Allahu Akbar! Allahu Akbar! Allahu Akbar!* God is great! *Ya Sirr us-Sirr!* O Secret of the Secret! There is nothing in me through which I do not commune with Him! I looked at my Lord with the eye of my heart and asked Him, "Who art Thou?" And He answered, "I am yourself."[6]

Haqq la ilaha illa'llah. Haqq la ilaha illa'llah. God is the truth. [Shattered beyond himself.] *Ana'l-Haqq!* I am the truth! I am He whom I love, and He who I love is I. We are the spirit of one, we are two spirits dwelling in one body. If thou seest me, thou seest Him, and if thou seest Him, thou seest us both.[7]

There is a stunned silence at such a proclamation.

HAZRAT INAYAT: The soul on its journey reaches a plane where it exclaims, "I am the truth."[8]

CONDEMNATION

Shaykh Junayd

This is too much for Shaykh Junayd, Hallaj's former teacher, who had dismissed his pupil.

JUNAYD: [Pointing his finger at Hallaj.] Have I not warned you not to proffer such sacrilege? You know well that to claim to be invested by the spirit of God is condemned by Islam as *hulul* (incarnationism — to claim to be invested by the spirit of God); and to put yourself on an equal footing with God is condemned as *shirk* (associationism — implying that one is a reality besides God). I dismiss you from my *silsilah*. What a gibbet you will befoul with your blood![9]

HALLAJ: I am a metaphor of God transported in man, not an analogy of man to God, nor a manifestation of God, nor an infusion of the spirit of God in a material receptacle.[10]

[To Junayd.] To condemn me, you will have to remove your Sufi robe and don the attire of a secular judge.

Junayd, in deference to custom, actually removes his Sufi robe and borrows a cape from a judge present at the scene.

SHAH NI'MATULLAH: Any disciple on the path of the ultimate attainment who all the other masters have cast away, liberate him from the bait and snare of the world and send him to me. Though by others he was rejected and turned away, I'll accept him in the holy poverty of God and make him drunk as befits him.[11]

Solon and the Students from *The Choicest Maxims and Most Priceless Sayings,*
Syria, 13th century.

SHABISTARI: When the veil is lifted from your eyes, nothing remains
of the schools and beliefs to which you resort. The whole religious
authority rests upon the antinomy "I and you"… You are the plurality
that becomes unity. You are the unity that becomes plurality. The
word "I" is not limited to man. To be able to declare that it only refers
to the soul, you need to have reached beyond time and space. "I" and
"you" are two horizons.[12]

MURID: [To Pir Vilayat.] What did the arguments that Shabistari used
to defy Junayd signify?

PIR VILAYAT: Shabistari is saying that though Junayd is supposed to
be a Sufi mystic, he is taking up the position of a secular judge who
has no idea about spiritual experience.

GILANI: Certain servants of the Lord are freed of their
legalistic intellects and are endowed with the "intellect of
intellects."[13]

SHAYKH AHMAD 'ALAWI: Our intelligences are made
drunk with the wine of love, as though we were mad, yet
mad we are not. Ours is an intelligence, a flawless jewel,
exquisite in beauty; it perceiveth naught but God.[14] For
ye are of God's spirit that entered into Adam, breath that
Gabriel breathed into Mary. Dance then in ecstasy and
pride and joy.[15]

Shaykh Ahmad 'Alawi.

IBN 'ARABI: If thou art veiled, in endeavoring to affirm [God's] transcendence thou affirmest in fact His likeness to other than Him. None is safe from the snare of making comparisons save him who companioneth the mystic and treadeth the path of those who realize the oneness. If thou examineth all that is, thou wilt find naught that is in addition to the oneness of the divinity.[16]

SHABISTARI: Listen to the call "I am God!" The one who knows reality, to whom unicity has been revealed, sees at the first glance the light of the Only Being.[17]

> *Now the imam of the Great Mosque of Cordoba is repeating,*
> *"Heaven and earth contain me not,*
> *but the heart of My faithful contains Me."*

RUMI: In me there is another by whom the eyes sparkle.[18] In love no more distinction between subject and object, lover and beloved.[19]

HE? I?

HALLAJ: [Kneeling.] You annihilated me out of myself into You. You made me near to myself so that I thought that I was You and You were me.[20] My spirit mixes with Your spirit in nearness and distance so that I am You and You are me.[21] Is it Thee? Is it me? That would be two gods. Far from me the affirmation of duality. [22]

IBN 'ARABI: [Kneeling, echoing Hallaj.] O God, O God! What is Thou and what is me? [23]

RUMI: With God two "I's" cannot find room. You say "I" and He says "I"… You die so that He may manifest Himself to you and duality may vanish.[24] God plays the game of "I" or "you" so that all "I's" and "you's" may merge into the one "I." To make a false claim is to say, "Thou art God (or He is God) and I am the servant." For in this way you are affirming your own existence, and duality is the necessary result. Hallaj had been annihilated, so those were the words of God. [25] When the spirit escaped from the "I" of the world, it became the "I."[26]

IBN 'ARABI: I have not found other than myself in my extinction and in my permanence.[27]

Herat's leading mystic, Khwaja 'Abdullah Ansari, reveals the gist of his experience.

ANSARI:
O God, there was a time when,
In search of Thee, I found myself;
But now that I am in search of
My self, I find Thee.[28]

Khwaja 'Abdullah Ansari

Hallaj then bursts forth once more with divine fervor, facing Junayd.

HALLAJ: How can you bear testimony to the divine unity if by the same token you are identifying yourself as the one who is affirming the testimony? As you say, "*Ashhadu* (I bear witness)," you are claiming to be the one who is proclaiming the credo. This is a contradiction![29]

Intrepid Shihab ud-Din Suhrawardi Maqtul (the Executed) cries out.

SUHRAWARDI: If you really lost yourselves, God cannot possibly seem to be a "Him." There are those who declare, "There is no God but God." These exclude all the "I's" other than the divine "I." There are those who declare, "There is no Him other than Him." It follows that no person other than Himself can call Him "Him," since all the "I's" derive from Him. There are those who declare, "There is no Thou but Thee." These are more advanced in that they do not invoke God in the third person as something absent, and furthermore, in that they deny any person who might claim to be a "thou." But whomsoever does the invoking confirms the otherness of God, and by that fact is guilty of *shirk*. Thus the only formula that fulfills the testimony is "There is none else but me."[30]

RUMI: Sometimes God makes the believer in the divine immanence a witness of His unity, and sometimes He diverts the believer in the divine transcendence from [God's] all-exclusiveness by revealing His multifarious forms.[31]

IBN 'ARABI: The manifestation of *huwa* (Him) only occurs when I am not anymore. If the *ana* (I) is still there when *huwa* manifests, then we have *anta* (Thou).[32]

Hallaj, having experienced the unity of God, speaks again.

HALLAJ: When a whole assembly is concentrating on a being, that being is more present than those concentrating upon him.

SUHRAWARDI: For the one overcome by love for the Divine Beloved, God is "Thee." Say, *"La anta illa anta* (There is no Thou but Thou)." But the one lost in divine love discovers God as the depth of himself. Say, *"La ana illa ana* (There is no I but I)!"[33]

A few in the assembly are outraged, others perplexed and rather confused. Some are reciting, "La hu illa hu." Others, "La anta illa anta." And there are those who feel in their consciousness ready to say, "La ana illa ana."

The citadel at Aleppo, Syria.

AM I GOD?

*I*BN 'ARABI:
[To Junayd.] If one says: "I am God,"
Then hearken to Him,
For it is God saying, "I am God!"
Not the servant

. . . .

For if thou hadst attained
To that to which He has attained,
Thou wouldst understand what He says

. . . .

And see what He sees.[34]

JUNAYD: [To Hallaj.] However, what you say is sheer apostasy. You are contradicting the words of the glorious Qur'an, *Allahu Ahad* (God is unique). In your immature mind, you claim to be confessors of unity, but true Muhammadan *tawhid* means that you preserve the stage of servantship while being immersed in the contemplation of God. Unification is the isolation of the eternal from the temporal.[37]

JILI: [Addressing Junayd.] Know that the perception of the Supreme Essence consists in that which thou knowest, in the path of divine intuition, that thou art Him and He is thee, without there being fusion of the two, the servant being the servant and the Lord being the Lord.[38]

IBN 'ARABI: There is in reality no union or division, for union is not possible except between two.[39] The profession of Islam, "*La ilaha illa'llah*," means it is all one.

RUMI: [Addressing Junayd.] People imagine that "*Ana'l-Haqq* (I am the truth)" is a presumptuous claim; whereas it is really a presumptuous claim to say "*Ana'l-'abd* (I am the slave of God)." The man who says "*Ana'l-'abd*," affirms two existences: his own and God's. But he who says "*Ana'l-Haqq*" has made himself nonexistent…. If he says, "I am drowning," he is not yet in the state of absorption.

THE BRUTALITY OF BIGOTRY

Ibn Da'ud

*T*HE JUDGE IBN DA'UD: [To Hallaj.] I condemn you beyond time and respite, and would condemn you forever, without respite, to be crucified.[41]

*The imam of Masjid-i Jami' in Herat
is reciting, "Thou are not assigned to manage
men's affairs." (Qur'an 17:54)*

RUMI: Whenever an ignorant judge holds his pen, there is a majdhub (a God-intoxicated dervish) on the scaffold.[39]

GILANI: Certain servants of the Lord are freed of their legalistic intellects *(uqul shar'iyya)* and are endowed with the "intellect of intellects" *('aql ul-'uqul).*[40]

JURAYRI: Ibn Da'ud is a jurist and it is in the nature of a jurist to reject Sufism.[41]

HAZRAT INAYAT: No one has entrance into the kingdom of God who had not been so crucified. Those who are given liberty by Him to act freely are nailed on the earth; and those who are free to act as they

The Royal Mosque (Masjid-i Shah) at Isfahan.

choose on the earth will be nailed in the heavens.[42] What can be said is that in suffering He Himself suffers; in rejoicing He Himself rejoices.[43]

HALLAJ: [Kneeling.] I have embarked on a vast ocean and my ship is shipwrecked. I shall die in the confession of the crucified.[44]

The faithful are repeating a hadith qudsi: *"I am with those whose hearts are broken for My sake."*

HALLAJ: [Answering.] Ecstasy is like a zephyr of joy that rises out of sadness.[45]

JAMI: In the contemplative's obliteration of the idiosyncrasies of the personality, there is pain in the divine touch. Suffering cleanses the contemplative, however, giving access in one's heart to God in His aloneness.[46]

DIE BEFORE DEATH
AND RESURRECT NOW

The judge comes again to the scene, addressing Hallaj.

*I*BN DA'UD: Moreover, I abjudicate that your body will be incinerated.

PIR VILAYAT: [To murid.] The judge decided to give Hallaj the worst possible treatment. Because Islam holds that the body must not be tampered with or incinerated because it is expected to resurrect after death, the judge thought that by incinerating his body, he would prevent Hallaj from resurrecting.

JUNAYD: Return to the state in which you were before you were involved in the state of becoming. Death is your access to the stage of this primordial life, which you should have sought in your search for unification without bringing in yourself. In your final stage you need to return to the state in which you were as you were in Him before you existed.[47]

The imam of al-Aqsa Mosque in Jerusalem is reciting,
"Remember: When thy Lord took from the children of Adam, from
their loins, their posterity and made them testify as to
themselves, 'Am I not your Lord?' and they said, 'Yea, we testify.'"
(Qur'an, 7:172)

JUNAYD: He made them testify as to themselves, "Am I not your Lord?" and they said, "Yea, we testify." He addressed them when they did not yet exist except insofar as He existentiated them. He existentiated them, encompassing them, witnessing them in the beginning when they were no thing apart from their eternal being, [in which] state they were from all pre-eternity.[48]

HALLAJ: My survival is not a simple return to pre-eternity. It is a reality that is imperceptible to the senses and beyond the reach of analogies.[49] [Kneeling.] You then bestowed on this present witness (myself, Hallaj) Your "I." How is it that You... who were present in my self after they had stripped me, who used my self to proclaim me myself, revealing the truth of my knowledge and my miracles, going back in my ascensions to the thrones of my pre-eternities to utter there the word itself which creates me, [You now wish] me to be seized, imprisoned, judged, executed, hung on the gibbet, my ashes to be thrown to the sandstorms that will scatter them, to the waves that will play with them. Now, the smallest particle [of my ashes], a grain of aloes (incense) [burned in this way to Your glory], assures to the [glorious] body of my transfigurations a more imposing foundation than that of immovable mountains![50]

MURID: What does Hallaj mean by the metaphor of the aloes?

PIR VILAYAT: [To murid.] Junayd suggests that through his death Hallaj will return back to his origin, whereas Hallaj holds that one does not just return to the way one was because something was gained by incarnating. To refer to the origin does not imply that we need to return to the same state. If God created this body, it must have been for a reason. Something is gained by it through its experience on earth, something that will be carried into everlastingness as the body gets transmuted in what is called resurrection. This is why according to Islam, to ensure resurrection the body must not be tampered with after death. But what happens if the body is not kept intact? Hallaj realized in a flash that to resurrect the physical body it had to be transmuted as incense.

Furthermore, why would God have created the world if He gains nothing by it? Remember Ibn 'Arabi's words: "In respect of Himself, He is independent of the worlds. But in respect of the most beautiful names (attributes), which demand the cosmos because of the possibility it offers in order for their effects to become manifest within it, He demands the existence of the cosmos."

> *The dervishes at Karbala repeat,*
> *"Die before death and resurrect now."*

RUMI: For tonight, the teeming world gives birth to the world everlasting.[51]

Sa'di

SA'DI: Of what use is a basket full of roses when one petal of the garden of roses is enough for you. The flower will die in a few days, while the garden will live forever![52]

MURID: I just don't understand what Hallaj did or said to earn such monstrous cruelty!

PIR VILAYAT: [To murid.] Out of respect for the divine transcendence, theology postulates a clear dividing line between God and man. God is of the nature of truth, *haqq*, which is by definition uncreated. According to the Qur'an, "God neither generates nor is generated." Man, therefore, is of a different nature, created. But Hallaj was upholding the divinity in man — a view more or less tacitly, mostly clandestinely, implied by most Sufi mystics — which is condemned by some mullahs (Islamic theologians) as the heretical doctrine of *hulul*. This rule is a safeguard against the claims of some teachers (present and past) who claim to be God.

Hallaj is ostensibly transported into another dimension. His great friend Ibn 'Ata comes to greet him. The assembly of Sufis stand still in rapt respect as the two greet each other in dervishi fashion, the arms crossed in a great X, bending low majestically.

HALLAJ: [To Ibn 'Ata.] *Ya 'Azim*, how gloriously God appears to me through you! My thought toward you has always been an expression of my love for God. I write, but this is not to you; in fact, it is my spirit to whom I write and therefore there is no need to send a letter. How is this possible? Because between the Divine Spirit and His lovers there is no disjunction owing to the difference between persons. This is why each letter coming from you brings to you my response, without a response being actually sent.... We are two spirits linked by our love of God.[55]

Ibn 'Ata

IBN 'ATA: When men of common parlance question us, we answer them with signs mysterious and dark enigmas; for the tongue of man cannot express so high a truth, whose span surpasses human measure. But my heart has known it, and has known of its rapture that thrilled and filled my body, every part. Seest thou not, these mystic feelings capture the very art of speech, as men who know vanquish and silence their unlettered foe.[54]

THOU ABANDONETH THOSE THOU LOVEST MOST

When the morning came, they led Hallaj from the prison, and a witness saw him walking proudly in his chains.

HALLAJ: [Reciting.] In that instant, I saw that I had been invited to the divine banquet, and that I was invited to drink from the chalice of the divine host, which was poison. Thus it falls to him who drinks wine with the Lion.[55]

Hallaj seems to collapse as he recalls Christ's words, "O take away this chalice," and again, his last words: "Why hast Thou abandoned me?" Then he arises as though overcome by a cosmic realization.

HALLAJ: Thy abandonment of me is a proof of Thy love, for Thou testest most those Thou lovest most.[56] [He pauses, then prays.] Forgive them. If You had revealed to them what You have revealed to me, they would not do what they are doing, and if You had concealed from me what You have concealed from them, I would not be able to undergo the ordeal that I am enduring. Praise be to You in whatsoever You do, praise be to You in whatsoever You will. [57]

[Turning toward the executioners.] It is your duty to kill me.

Peri holding a cup.

They led him then to the esplanade, where they cut off his hands and feet after having flogged him with 500 lashes of the whip. Then he was hoisted up onto the cross, and one could hear him on the gibbet talking ecstatically with God.

Hallaj in front of the executioner.

HALLAJ: O my God, here am I in the dwelling place of my desires, where I contemplate Your marvels.[58]

As Hallaj was hanging on the cross, Shibli, the poet who disagreed with Hallaj's divulging the secrets of his love for God, spoke.

SHIBLI: Did I not warn you not to receive a guest at night?[59]

PIR VILAYAT: [To the murids standing in witness.] That guest was God. Shibli accused Hallaj of revealing the secret of his love for God.

SHIBLI: [Asking Hallaj.] What is Sufism?

HALLAJ: The lowest degree one needs for attaining it is the one that you behold.

Shibli

SHIBLI: What is the highest degree?

HALLAJ: It is out of reach for you, but tomorrow you will see; for it is part of the divine mystery that I have seen it and that it remains hidden to you.[60]

GHAZALI: The speech of lovers in the state of intoxication should be concealed and not spread about.[61] What is more, not every mystery is to be unveiled and divulged, and not every reality is to be presented and disclosed. Indeed, "to divulge the mystery of Lordship is unbelief."[62]

'AYN UL-QUDAT HAMADANI:
Most of those called the "faithful" or the
"Believers" are in reality idolaters

. . . .

The master of the religious law knows
By the light of prophesy that madmen
Must be put in chains; the religious law
Has been made the chain of these
Maddened wayfarers of reality.
Those burned up by love are melancholy,

And melancholy is related to madness
And madness is on the road to infidelity.[63]

'Ayn ul-Qudat Hamadani

GHAZALI:
Glory to the one
Who has liberated the hearts of His saints
Of their concupiscence for the world
And its treachery,
Who purified their heart of any thought
Except of that of His presence
And chose their hearts
For His glorification on earth,
Then revealed Himself to them
Through His names and attributes,
So that their hearts were kindled
By the contact with the flares of His cognizance,
Then revealed to them the majesty of His face
So that their hearts were consumed
By the flames of His love,
Then eluded the grasp of their hearts
By the power of His majesty
So that they wandered in the perilous deserts
Of His sublime magnificence.[64]

Ghazali

*The next morning, they took Hallaj down from the gibbet and
dragged him forth to behead him. A witness said,
"I heard him cry out then, saying in a very high voice:
'All that matters for the ecstatic is that his only one bring
him to His oneness!'"*[67]

PIR VILAYAT: Instead of seeking a long-awaited refuge from agony, Hallaj knew that this ordeal was the fulfillment of his life's purpose so that it should be God alone who attests to His ultimate unity. By offering itself up to God in devotion, Hallaj's body participated across the threshold of death in the process of resurrection in the ultimate affirmation of the Islamic *shahada*, "La illaha illa'llah (There is none else but God)."

*The imam of the Mosque of Baghdad is reciting,
"The hour of death is not far."
(Qur'an 42:16)*

*Hallaj reflects upon those suffering agony in their bodies and
their wish for death to come soon as a relief.*

HALLAJ: Those who do not believe in the final hour call for its coming…[66] but the faithful await it with a reverential fear, for they know that it is the moment of truth. (Qur'an 42:17)

These were his last words.

GLORIFICATION

GLORIFICATION

Sensing the divine presence, all those in the assembly betake themselves to prayer. All thoughts and hearts turn toward the Ka'aba.

As the Sufis in unison stand, bend, kneel, and prostrate, some of the fervid words of the prayer are overheard:

Allahu Akbar! (God is great!)

Subhana Rabbi al-'Azim! (Glory to my Lord, the Magnificent!)

Sami' Allahu liman hamida;
Rabbana laka'l-hamd!
(God has heard the one who praises Him;
Praise be to Thee, our Lord!)
Subhana Rabbi al-A'la! (Glory to my Lord, the Most High!)

Ashhadu an la ilaha illa'llah, ashhadu an Muhammadan Rasul Allah!
(I bear witness that there is no God but God; I bear witness that Muhammad is the messenger of God!)

O Allah! Shower Thy blessings on
Our leader Muhammad and his descendants
As Thou showered Thy blessings
On our leader Abraham and his descendants.
Thou art the Praiseworthy and the Glorious!

O Allah, I have been unjust,
And none grants forgiveness
Against sins but Thou.
Therefore, forgive me with the
Forgiveness that comes from Thee
And have mercy upon me.
Verily Thou art the Forgiver,
The Merciful!

As-Salam 'alaykum wa Rahmat Allah wa Barakatuhu!
(Peace be upon you and the mercy of Allah!)

IBN 'ARABI: My God, Thou hast desired me; consequently I am the
desired one and Thou the desirer. But be Thyself the desired one in
me and make me the desirer.[1]

HAZRAT INAYAT: The faithful does not only pray to God, but he prays
before God and in the presence of God.... Once the imagination has
helped man to bring the presence of God before him, the God in his

own heart is awakened. Then before he utters a word, it is heard by God. When he is praying in a room he is not alone; he is there with God. Therefore, God to him is not in the highest heaven but next to him, before him, and in him. Heaven to him is on earth, and the earth for him is Heaven. No one to him is then so living as God or so intelligible as God, and the names and forms before him are all covered under him. Every word of prayer he says is a living word. It not only brings him blessing, but also brings blessings to all those around him.[2]

IBN SINA: It is prayer which causes the human soul to resemble the heavenly abodes eternally worshipping absolute truth… for worship is knowledge…. The real nature of prayer is therefore to know God in His uniqueness whose essence is infinitely exalted and whose qualities are infinitely holy. The outward part of the prayer is prescribed by the religious law…. This outward or disciplinary part is connected with the body because it is composed of certain postures such as recitation, genuflection, and prostration…. They act as controlling the body to bring it in tune with the harmony of the universe. The lawgiver prescribed prayer for the body as an outward symbol for that other prayer. As for the second or inward part, or truth of prayer, this is to contemplate God with a pure heart and a spirit abstracted and purified of all desires. This part does not follow the path of bodily numbers or physical actions, but rather the art of pure thoughts and eternal spirits…[3]

[He pauses.] Man can reach God only as far as his imagination can take him.[4] The first thing a believer does is to imagine. He imagines that God is the Creator, and tries to believe that God is the Sustainer, and he makes an effort to think that God is a friend, and an attempt to feel that he loves God. But if this imagination is to become a reality, then exactly as one feels for one's earthly beloved sympathy, love, and attachment, so one must feel the same [emotions] for God.[5]

Man praying in the courtyard of the Karaouine Mosque in Fez, Morocco.

PIR VILAYAT: The being of God comes through these beings when they realize that their personalities — their selves — are expressions of the being of God waiting to manifest.

THE PROPHET MUHAMMAD'S PRESENCE IS FELT

After the prayers, the voices are still reverberating over the Ka'aba as the faithful repeat, "Ashhadu an la ilaha illa'llah; Ashhadu an Muhammadan rasulullah (I bear witness that there is no God but God and Muhammad is His Prophet)."

A voice is heard resonating through infinite outreaches of space.

'Uways Qarani, for whom the Prophet Muhammad was always present no matter where he was, recognizes the voice.

QARANI: It is the voice of the Prophet (peace and blessings be upon him).

GHAZALI: How do you know?

'Uways Qarani

QARANI: I always knew how he felt, and he always knew how I felt. It seems strange how few Muslims recognize the voice of the Prophet (peace and blessings be upon him)!

Hazrat 'Ali is now on his knees, placing his index fingers first on his lips, then on his eyes in the Muslim custom of showing reverential affection and devotion for the Prophet of Islam. The whole assembly follows.

ALL: O Lord, bless Muhammad and his family. Salute to you, O Prophet. Peace, mercy, and blessing of God be upon you. Peace be upon you and the devout followers of God. The peace and mercy of God be upon you.

*Still under the spell of Hallaj's rapture, they undergo what the Sufis
call a state of* fana fi'llah, *losing oneself in God.*

*Dervishes at the Dargah of Baba Farid at
Pak Pattan, Pakistan, prostrate, saying, "I die for Thee,"
then rise, saying, "I live for Thee."*

*Dervishes at the Dargah of Shaykh Shihab ud-Din Suhrawardi
at Aleppo, Syria, prostrate, saying, "I die in Thee,"
then rise, saying, "I live in Thee."*

Maulana Jalal ud-Din intervenes.

RUMI: Thou didst contrive this "I" and "we" in order to play the game
of worship with Thyself, that all "I's" and "thou's" might become one
soul and at last be submerged in the Beloved.[6]

*The cry of "Ya Quddus! Ya Quddus! Ya Quddus! (O Holy!)"
spreads throughout the saintly company in the gigantic
assembly hall. More and more Sufis are gathering from all parts of
Planet Earth and elsewhere. One can distinguish innumerable
shaykhs, murshids, pirs, dervishes, madhubs and fakirs of
many different Sufi* silsilahs:
*Chishtiyya, Suhrawardiyya, Qadiriyya, Naqshbandiyya,
Shattariyya, Ni'matullahiyya, Kubrawiyya, Yasawiyya,
Nurbakhshiyya, Zahabiyya, Haydariyya, Rifa'iyya, Khalwatiyya,
Mawlawiyya, Shamsiyya, Bektashiyya,
Badawiyya, Shadhiliyya.*

*"Ya Hu, Ya Hu! (O He, O He!)" cry the entire assembly of Sufis.
They call out the many names of God.*

*"Ya Sami', ya Kalam!
(O Thou who art the Listener and the Word!)"
cries Shah Ni'matullah Wali.*

*"Ya Majid!" murmurs Ibn ul-Farid of Egypt.
"All glory originates in Thee!"*

View of Ankara, Turkish School, 18th century.

"Ya 'Azim! *Thou art the glory which I manifest,*
and Thou, Thy glory manifests in me as majesty,"
cries Mu'in ud-Din Chishti.
"Ya Wajid, Ya Mawjud!"

"Ya 'Alim! *Thou art the meaningfulness behind all situations!"*
cries Kalabadhi.

"Ya Khabir!" *cries Baha ud-Din Naqshband.*
"The Intelligence becomes consciousness in creation!"

"Ya Batin!" *cries Bibi Jamil.*
"The divine reality is veiled in the unknown!"

"Ya Zahir!" *exclaims Ibn 'Arabi.*
"Grasp what transpires behind what appears!"

Simnani calls out,
"Ya Nur ul-Anwar *(O Light of Lights)!*
Ya Nur ul-'Aql *(O Light of Intelligence)!*
It is Thee that transpires."

"Ya Nur Ya Munawwar!
In all forms and colors, as in a rainbow, are reflected in the mirror,"
says Nuri.

"Ya Quddus! Ya Ruh ul-Quds!
Thou art Holy Spirit quickening all beings!"
says Ruzbihan Baqli.

"Ya Hayy! *(O Life-Giver!)*
The breath of Thy spirit triggers off all life,"
says Kalimullah Jahanabadi.

"Ya Muhyi!
Thou regenerate the life energy when it tarries,"
says Jabir ibn Hayyan.

Having communicated regardless of time and space,
the minds of the whole assembly are elevated once more
into pondering the ineffible, which Hallaj espied when
stalking time beyond becoming. He espied the state of God
in the primary state
that the Sufis call azaliyat *(pre-eternity).*

IBN 'ARABI: In Thy eternity the "without beginning" and "without end" coincide.[7]

HALLAJ: In His pre-eternity God found Himself in Himself.

"Ya Samad! *(O Eternal One!)"*
cries Affifi.

"Ya Qayyum! *(O Self-Subsisting One!)"*
exclaims Hujwiri.

"Ya Akhir! *(O Thou who art the Last!)"*
says Gisudaraz.

HALLAJ: God found Himself in Himself.

"Ya Ahad! *(O Only One!)"*
cries Sana'i.

HAZRAT INAYAT: In the beginning, when there was no earth, nor heaven, there was eternal awareness — a silent, inactive state of being, a state of unawakened Intelligence. Within it, there awakened to its own nature the awareness of its own existence unlimited by form and space.[8]

HALLAJ: Then in the solitude of oneness the emotion of love arose.

"Ya Wahid! *(O Unique One!)"*
exclaims 'Alawi.

Hazrat Fatima repeats, "'Ishq Allah ma'bud Allah!
(God is love, the Lord of whom I am the servant!)"

HALLAJ: He contemplated His attributes in their perfection one by one.

"Ya Kamal! *(O Perfect One!)" cries Sa'adi.*

HALLAJ: Then He sparked a form...

"Ya Mubdi! *(O Originator!)"*
cries Abu Bakr ul-Warraq.

"Ya Khaliq! *(O Creator!)"*
exclaims Nizam ud-Din Aurangabadi.

HALLAJ: Then He sparked a person...

Muhasibi repeats,
"Dhu'l-Jalal wa'l-Ikram! *(The Lord of power and splendor!)"*

HALLAJ: Then He glorified him...

"Ya Hamid! *(O Praiseworthy!)"*
cries Yunus Emre.

Shah Ni'matullah Wali calls out,
"Al-hamdu li'llah! *(Praise be to God!)"*

HALLAJ: And He made him the elect.

"Ya Badi'! *(O Incomparable One!)"*
murmurs Jahanara.

THE ZEPHYR FROM THE DESERT

As everyone sits in silence, pondering over those words, an uncanny sound fills the hall. Some think they are hearing the call for prayer of the muezzin, accompanied by fleeting vocalizations as in the style of the Iranian Shi'ites. Others think they hear gongs, bells, or even choirs as from the churches of the Syrian monks of the desert. Still others think they hear odd intonations — vibrations echoing throughout the spheres, such as have never been heard on earth.

Another presence is felt. There are no visible signs, except everything seems to be surprisingly clear. A wind from the desert is blowing into a gale. It sounds like the whistling of the waves of the atmosphere of outer space churned by the planets. The green aura-like figure of Khidr-Elijah, the mysterious appearance in the desert who makes himself known to those who get lost, is floating across the hall. With an almost inhuman voice, it speaks.

Khidr-Elijah

HIDR:
   If you wish,
   I will lead you to the waters of life,
   But if you question My guidance,
   You are on your own.
   He who tries to preserve his life
   Will lose it
   And he who relinquishes it,
   Finds it,
   Transmuted and transfigured!
   We inspired these words
   To Lord Isa, *Ruh Allah*.

PIR VILAYAT: [Explaining to the murids and inquirers.] *Ruh Allah* (the Spirit of God) is the Muslim name for Jesus.

THE ESOTERIC TRADITION
BEHIND THE EXOTERIC

Salman Pak Farsi, who had traveled across the desert to meet the Prophet and communicate to him the secrets of the Magi, speaks.

FARSI: Know ye that the Prophet (peace be upon him) gave sentences to the many and maxims to the chosen ones.

Salman Pak Farsi

ABU SA'ID IBN ABI'L-KHAYR: The seven sevenths of the Qur'an Sharif are "O, apostle! Deliver the message that hath been sent down to Thee." (Qur'an 5:71) And the eighth seventh is "He revealed unto His servant that which He revealed." (Qur'an 3:10)[9] It is this revelation that is communicated to the Sufis in their *muraqaba* (meditations).

RUMI: The blind religious are in a dilemma, for the champions on either side stand firm: Each party is delighted with its own path. Love alone can end their quarrel. Love alone comes to the rescue when you cry for help against their arguments.[10]

RUZBIHAN BAQLI: In their misguidedness, they killed some and burned others to death.[11] They thought it was faith and did not know that it was oppression. They gave these pure ones into the hands of the impure mobs.[12]

Ruzbihan Baqli

HAZRAT INAYAT: Man always reasons with another; but it is not a dispute between reason and no reason, it is a dispute between two reasons contrary to one another.[13] When one rises above what is called reason one reaches that reason which is at the same time contradictory. Yet beyond this dilemma there is always a reason behind a reason — a higher reason. And when one arrives at this higher reason one begins to "unlearn," as it is called by the mystics, all that one has once learned. Very often intellectualism explains a knowledge formed by reasons, most of them of rigid character. The fine reason is subtle;

the finer the reason, the less it can be explained in words.[14] A mystic does not look at reasons as everybody else does, because he sees that the first reason that comes to his mind is only a cover over another reason which is hidden behind it.[15] He does not see things through the reason he has learned from the world, but he begins to see the reason of all reasons, the reason which is covered by ordinary reasoning.[16]

Prince Dara Shikuh, a Sufi initiate who pointed out the parallels between Hinduism and Islam, joins in.

Prince Dara Shikuh

DARA SHIKUH: The power of the commonality between Hinduism and Islam is like the meeting of oceans. The Indian mystics do not disown the unity of God. The Vedas are an ocean of monotheism in conformity with the Holy Qur'an. The sentences in the Holy Qur'an are literally to be found therein. The hidden book is a precursor to it. Islam and Hinduism are both galloping toward [God].[17]

The imam of the great mosque of Mecca recites, "The prototype of the glorious Qur'an is in the sacred volume. It must not be touched except by the pure. It is a revelation by the Lord of the Universe." (Qur'an 56:77-80)

HAZRAT INAYAT: The wise in olden times said to those who were not capable of imagination, "Here is a statue of God." Those who worshipped these statues — the Chinese, the Greeks, the Hindus — were they mistaken? No, each person's God is as he looks upon Him.[18]

SHABISTARI: If the [Muslim] only knew: He sees in idols only the visible creature, not the truth hidden in the idol.[19]

Kabir, who rose above the differences between Hinduism and Islam by pointing out their common denominator, enters the discussion.

KABIR:

Are you longing for me?

I am in the next seat.

My shoulder is against yours.

You will not find me in *stupas*,

Not in Indian shrine rooms,

Nor synagogues, nor in cathedrals,

Not in masses, nor *kirtans*,

Not in legs winding around your own neck,

Nor in eating nothing but vegetables.

When you really look for me, you will see me
   instantly —

You will find me in the tiniest house of time.[20]

Kabir

I don't know what sort of a God we have been talking about.

The caller calls in a loud voice to the Holy One at dusk.

Why? Surely the Holy One is not deaf.

He hears the delicate anklets that ring on the feet of an insect as it
   walks.

Go over and over your beads, paint weird designs on your forehead,

Wear your hair matted, long, and ostentatious,

But when deep inside you there is a loaded gun, how can you have
   God?[21]

Sufi Saint of the 16th century, Shaykh Salim.

MURID: [To Pir Vilayat.] Is that not injurious to both Hindus and Muslims?

PIR VILAYAT: It is bold — but its irony is intended to diffuse the offense.

GOD THE FATHER?

MURID: Something has been bothering me all this time. I can see how Muslims have difficulty in accepting the idolatry of the Hindus or the divine inheritance of Christ in the Christian faith. And yet we are trying to tolerate one another's beliefs for the sake of unity. How can we bridge these differences and affirm a common ground in the diversity of religious tenants?

HAZRAT INAYAT: Unity is not uniformity.

> *Some dervishes repeat, "Lam yalid wa lam yulad*
> *(He does not beget nor is He begotten)."*

MURID: But isn't Christ the son of God?

> *Maimonides, the famous Jewish philosopher who received guidance*
> *from the Muslim philosopher Farabi, steps forward.*

MAIMONIDES: The term *yalod* means, "to bear," as in "They have born him children." "And Adam begat a son in his own likeness, in his form." The word was next used in a figurative sense. The term yalod further denotes "to bring forth," changes in the process of time, as though they were things that were born: "...for thou knowest not what a day may bring forth." (Prov. 27:1)[22]

Maimonides

HAZRAT INAYAT: There is a great difference in the beliefs and opinions of people about the immaculate birth of Jesus. The truth is that when the soul arrives at the point of understanding the truth of life in its collective aspect, he realizes that there is only one father, and that is God; this world out of which all the names and forms have been created is the mother.

PIR VILAYAT: The incarnationist dogma of Christianity was decided by a small minority of church fathers at the Council of Nycea. At the Council of Nycea there were discussion as to the divine and human natures of God, and it was decided that He was truly God and truly man. The word *father* may be used as signifying an archetypal father figure — for example, an old woman calling a young Catholic priest "Father." While a son or a daughter may inherit some of the qualities or defects of his or her parent, the Sufis refer to a different relationship between the divine nature (the archetype) and the human nature (the exemplar). The Sufis strive to foster the relationship between God as archetype and us humans as exemplars in order to perfect ourselves to such an extent that these exemplars manifest, or actuate, the features of the divine model as perfectly as possible, as represented by the concept of the perfect man.

MURID: But don't we have here two conflicting points of view?

INQUIRER: I find the resurrection of Christ equally puzzling, especially since the stone had been removed. It is not unlikely that Joseph of Arimathea had the body retrieved. Today many people do not rely upon the belief imposed upon them by organized religion.

HAZRAT INAYAT: If the resurrection merely meant that Christ rose again after his death, it would be a story to be believed or disbelieved. Its lesson is much greater: It refers to the resurrection from this mortal life to immortality.[23]

The Shroud of Turin, said to carry an imprint of Christ after his crucifixion.

INQUIRER: So if I understand correctly, according to Prophet Muhammad, Christ occupies a special place among the prophets because he was quickened by the spirit of God.

THE IMAM OF MASJID UZ-ZAYTUN IN FEZ, MOROCCO: We have accorded precellence to some prophets over others.... We granted Jesus, son of Mary, with clear evidence. We have quickened him with the Holy Spirit. (Qur'an 2:253) His name "the Messiah, son of Mary" figures in this world and the other among those close to God (3:45)... the chosen one has already come to you. (4:170) God elevated Him to Himself. (4:158)

Ascent of the Prophet, from *Khamsah* by Nizami, Shiraz, Iran, 1410.

HAZRAT INAYAT: Yes, the Prophet brings a religion, but that is not all. What he really brings on earth is the living God.

INQUIRER: But what then is the position of Prophet Muhammad?

HAZRAT INAYAT: Prophet Muhammad, the seal of the prophets, gave the final statement of divine wisdom: "None exists but Allah." This message fulfilled the aim of prophetic mission.[24] The prophecy of Muhammad was, "Now that all the world has received the message through a man who is subject to all limitations and conditions of human life, the message will in the future be given without claim."[25]

Every soul has the source of the divine message within himself. This is the reason why there is no need for mediation, for an intercessor as a savior between man and God.[26]

The Standard Bearers of the Caliph's guard, illustration from *Maqamat of* Hariri, painted by Yahya ibn Mahmud Wasiti, Bhagdad, 1237.

Salman Pak Farsi interjects, referring to a hadith.

FARSI: The Prophet (peace be upon him) said that on the day of resurrection, God will manifest Himself to the creatures in the forms that they themselves refuted, announcing "I am your Lord." In the face of this unfamiliar apparition, they will seek refuge in their own representation of God. Then God will appear in that representation, and then they will believe that indeed it is Him.

HAZRAT INAYAT: Therefore the people of that part of the world who have acknowledged the Hebrew prophets do not for instance recognize avatars such as Rama and Krishna and Shiva, simply because they cannot find these names in their scriptures. The same thing occurs in the other part of humanity which does not count Abraham, Moses, and Jesus among its *devatas*, as it does not find those names written in the legends with which it is familiar.

IBN 'ARABI: The God who is in a faith is the God whose form the heart contains, who discloses Himself to the heart in such a way that the heart recognizes Him. Thus the eye sees only the God of the faith.[27]

THE UNITY OF WORLD RELIGIONS

The Sufis at Ajmer are repeating a **hadith:**
"He discloses Himself in the form of beliefs."

RUMI:

I adore not the cross nor the crescent, I am not a Geber nor a
Jew.

East nor West, land nor sea is my home; I have kin not with
angel nor gnome.

. . . .

I am wrought not of fire nor of foam, I am shaped not of dust
nor of dew.

I was born not in China afar, not in Saqsin and not in
Bulghar.

Not in India where five rivers are, nor Iraq nor Khorasan I
grew.

Not in this world nor that world I dwell; not in Paradise,
neither in Hell;

Not from Eden and Rizwan I fell, not from Adam my lineage
I drew. [28]

My place is the placeless, my trace is the traceless,

'Tis neither body nor soul, for I belong to the soul of the
Beloved. [29]

I have put duality away, I have seen that the two worlds
are one.

One I seek, one I know, one I see, one I call.[30]

HAFIZ:

I am in love with every church and mosque and temple
And any kind of shrine
Because I know it is there
That people say the different names
Of the one God.[31]

IBN 'ARABI:
My heart is capable of every form:
A cloister for the monk, a temple
  for idols,
A pasture for gazelles, the votary's
  Ka'aba,
The tables of the Torah, the Qur'an.
Love is the creed I hold [32]

HAZRAT INAYAT: The faithful of different religions know God according to the form in which they conceive Him, not in the form in which another religion conceives Him. The message of our time collects all

A group of Sufi saints, 1760.

forms in one, universal form to which people are not accustomed, so that the followers of all religions may worship at the same time.[33]

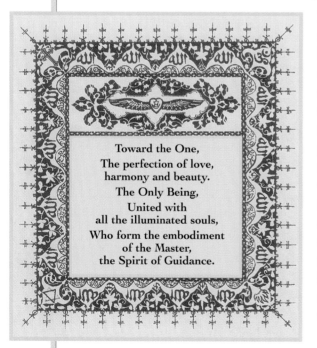

Toward the One,
The perfection of love,
harmony and beauty.
The Only Being,
United with
all the illuminated souls,
Who form the embodiment
of the Master,
the Spirit of Guidance.

HAZRAT INAYAT: The aim of the Sufi message is to unite [humanity] in a world kinship beyond the boundaries of caste, creed, race, nation, or religion, realizing the whole of humanity is one single body and that all nations, communities, and races are the different organs. The happiness and well-being of each of them is the happiness and well-being of the whole body.[34] [Sufism] is the answer to the cry of [all] humanity. Sufism respects all religions and their prophets, saints, and masters, encouraging people to value the gift of their religion by discovering its deeper meaning. The purpose of the message is the awakening of humanity to the divinity in man.[35]

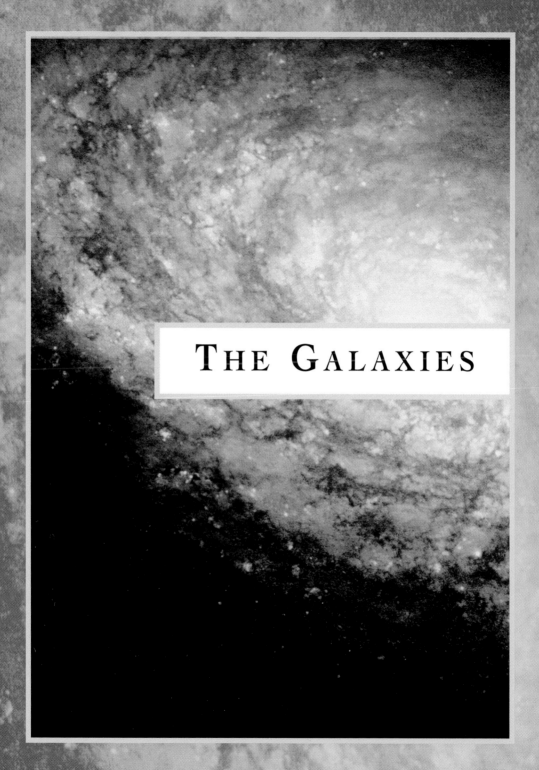

THE GALAXIES

The Blue Mosque at Tabriz, Iran.

THE ARCHANGELS OF LIGHT

The rumble of the hoofs of Prince Hurakhsh's 70,000 winged steeds is heard grazing the palace roofs as he moves, circling vast horizons to survey his immense kingdom.

SUHRAWARDI: The venerable Prince Hurakhsh, the most sublime of those who have assumed a body, invested with the divine countenance, sparkles rapture in the sphere of Hurqalya. Sometimes he appears in human form, sometimes as the sun, sometimes as a constellation, sometimes as a work of art or an icon. It is he who confers light upon those who meditate upon the celestial spheres.[1]

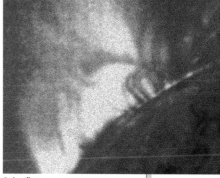

Solar flares.

[After pausing for a moment of contemplation.] Thereupon the light of the spheres dawns upon the horizon of the initiate, conferring upon him the sovereignty of the angels, of which the sidereal constellations are the projections and which in turn are governed by these. The one who becomes invested by the incandescence of the spheres becomes a magnificent king, manifesting the splendor of the angelic spheres, surrounded with respect, and invested with wisdom, perfection, and prosperity.[2]

The rafters and windows of the great assembly hall shake with a din like the horrendous thunder of millions of contrabasses and as many gongs, accompanied by the shriek of piccolo flutes and cymbals, and supplemented by countless sounds from other dimensions of space, conveying to all present the semblance of the symphony of the spheres.

SUHRAWARDI: Hail to the pilgrims knocking at the gates of the high naves of the great halls of light, with righteousness and resolve, for behold the angels hastening to meet you, greeting you with the salutations of the celestial realm, and guiding you toward the Orient of Light![3]

RUMI: Enough of metaphor — all I want is burning! Burning! Burning![4] The divine sun has veiled Himself in man.[5] To us, this day of days, He has unveiled Himself if we have the strength to face Him.... For thence arises the appearance of number and plurality.... Fix thy gaze upon the light and thou art delivered from the dualism inherent in the finite body.[6]

Shams-i Tabriz comes forth.

SHAMS-I TABRIZ: This is my secret: I have been invested with the fire of Prince Hurakhsh. If you have the courage to face the glare of Prince Hurakhsh, all who face you will be set aflame.

Abraham surrounded by flames, from *Anthology of Iskandar,* Shiraz, Iran, 1410.

Sculptures from Srirangam Temple, Tamil Nadu, India.

PRINCE HURAKHSH: Beware that you do not confuse the light that sets off all creation from the fire that spreads destruction. Know ye, humans, that your thoughts affect My radiance, just as My radiance affects your consciousness.

As Prince Hurakhsh emerges cosmically from a diaphanous shroud of crimson, terra cotta, sepia, turquoise, and purple, he now reveals himself as a triumphant being, sovereign, rather than just an impersonal luminary — the archangel of the sun, likened to a galaxy.

In his wake, he seems to open a channel, a giant pathway of vacated space, linking universes of various subtle fabrics — untold spheres beyond our compass — and ensuring the interconnection of all levels of being in the cosmic harmony.

The vast hall opens up into the city, and further cities, and then into the starry sky, expanding into the galaxies. It is midnight, but the night is flooded by blinding light. A dazzling outburst of light gleams upon the faces of the God-intoxicated Sufis, stirring the their auras into a flurry of multicolored flashes, like huge fireworks. Not in a thousand sunrises or sunsets has the sun shown forth such glory!

Hallaj, once again spirited from the worlds of light with a message to the humans on Planet Earth, speaks.

HALLAJ: The light of Thy being has dawned upon the horizon of my being, and there will be no sunset![7]

SUHRAWARDI: Deliver the people of light; lead the light to the Light.[8]

IBN SINA: It happens that men who have isolated themselves from society emigrate toward God.[9]

SUHRAWARDI: Then the light of dawn rises upon them.[10] Once the divine lights are dispersed within a man, he is clothed in a robe of sovereignty and majesty.[11]

The Last Man by John Martin.

THE MESSAGE OF THE GALAXIES

Shihab ud-Din Suhrawardi, the young initiate who had revived the
ancient tradition of the priest-kings, turns facing the full glare.
Here is the epitome of all that he had ever searched for: the light of the
archangels of light, from which we derive the light of
our intelligence, manifesting right here to the gaze of all as the
archangel of the sun.

From the *Commentary of the Apocalypse* by the Spanish Monk Beatus, dated 1109.

SUHRAWARDI: Be not surprised when you learn in the treatise of the ancient sages that there is a world endowed with dimensions and extensions other than the physical world, not to be confused with the sphere of pure intelligence or the sphere of the soul. It is a world in which there are innumerable cities — two of which were mentioned by the Prophet under the names Jabalqa and Jabarsa. Sometimes spiritual pilgrims discover these and find in them the fulfillment of their nostalgia.[12]

The Sufi dervishes at the tomb of Suhrawardi
are repeating, "Ya Nur (O Light), Ya Munawwar
(Radiant One)!"

PIR VILAYAT: The planet is an emanation of the sun — the body of Prince Hurakhsh — which further derives from the outburst of life in the galaxies and clusters of cosmic stardust where new life emerges incessantly. Our bodies carry not only the genes of Prince Hurakhsh but that of the universe of stars. But imagine — we inherit from the intelligence of the spheres, the galaxies.

RUMI: A million galaxies are a little scum on that shoreless sea[13]…We came whirling out of nothingness, scattering stars like dust; the stars made a circle and in the middle we dance…. Turning and turning [the dance] sunders all attachment… every atom turns bewildered… and it is only God circling Himself.[14] Every form you see has its archetype in the placeless world. If the form perished, no matter, since its original is everlasting.[15] God has placed a ladder before us. We must climb it.[16]

SUHRAWARDI: Our souls are born out of spheres of light, originating in the *Xvarnah*, the flamboyant majesty of the crown of the King of the Universe in the Orient of Light. Each flare of effulgence gives rise to a new hypostase of light, each representing a different order of being, starting from the *Anwar Qahira* (the archangels of light) reverberating through the spheres of stellar angels. Each receives its light from the beings preceding it in the hierarchy of light behind the universe of matter, until all this light breaks up into those sparks that represent the *fravarti*, our human souls.[17]

A spiral galaxy taken by the Hubble space telescope.

RUMI:

Beyond the stars are stars in which there is no combust,
Stars moving in other heavens, not the seven heavens known to all.
Stars immanent in the light of God, neither joined to each other nor
    separate.[18]

> *The emotion generated by this infinite outreach resonates through the murids, gradually infiltrating into the hearts of the denizens of Planet Earth.*

PIR VILAYAT: The key to making sense of life is to be found in the portentous event wherein that global being we call God, endowed with intelligence, will, and love, is recurrently fashioning Herself into a plethora of beings. Each carries the potential of that Being but customizes it, thus diversifying it in a unique way. The universe actuating in the cosmos offers the gift of freedom to each fragment of Itself. From this arises the dichotomy between joy and suffering. On one hand, joy floods the cosmos as the splendor inherent in the universe is configured into a panoply of meaningful structures catalyzed by the ecstasy that triggers off creativity. On the other hand, the price for the gift of freedom is its abuse, and the trail of suffering, injustice, tyranny, terror, and agony that come from creatures abusing their freedom. To make sense of this enigma, one must reverse one's personal vantage point and try seeing everything from the antipodal vantage point — God's.

Angel Gabriel, Syria or Egypt, around 1375–1425.

HAZRAT INAYAT: The pure consciousness has, so to speak, gradually limited itself by entering into vehicles such as the mind and the body. Yet the divine mind is completed after manifestation. The divine mind is made of his own creation. Divinity resides in humanity; it is also the outcome of humanity. The soul is God, but man has a body and mind of his own. The planet has culminated into human beings.[19] There is a gradual awakening of matter to become conscious. Through the awakening of matter to increased consciousness, matter becomes conscious; man gains a conviction that frees him from the earth. In matter life unfolds, discovers, and realizes the consciousness that has been... buried in it for thousands of years.[20] The same God, so little of whose perfection manifested in the plant, arises again and again trying to emerge as perfect as possible in the midst of human imperfection. As the seed is sufficient in itself and capable of producing another plant, so man is the product of all the planes, spiritual and material, and yet it is in him alone that shines forth that which caused the whole — that primal intelligence, the seed of existence — God.[21] The collective working of many minds as one single idea, and the activity of the whole world, are governed by the intelligence of the planet and unlock the doors opening up into a glorious future. The thought of any person is the thought of the entire human race. The whole universe has contributed to the way humanity thinks today.[22]

The experience of every soul becomes the experience of the divine mind. Not knowing that God experiences this life through man, [we are] seeking for Him somewhere else.

The purpose of this whole creation is fulfilled in the attainment of that perfection which is for a human being to attain.[23] The purpose of life is fulfilled in rising to the greatest heights and in diving to the deepest depths of life, in widening one's horizons, in penetrating life in all its spheres, in losing oneself, and in finding oneself in the end.[24] The purpose of every soul is that for which the whole creation has been striving and it is the fulfillment of that purpose that is called God-consciousness.[25]

> *When the unreality of life pushes against my heart,*
> *Its door opens to the reality.*

Bibliographical References

The author has translated all foreign-language texts; some passages have been paraphrased for this publication. Cites to the work of Hazrat Inayat Khan refer to the database containing his complete work, housed at the International Secretariat of the Sufi Order. They will be able to guide you through his work, as well as give you details of books he authored, including *Gayan Vadan Nirtan* (Sufi Order Publications 1980), *Sangatha Series 1* (Sufi Order Publications), and *The Flower Garden of Inayat Khan* (East-West Publication, 1978). They will also help you with further information on the activities of the Sufi Order International.

Sufi Order International Secretariat
North American Secretariat
P. O. Box 30065
Seattle, WA 98103

T: (206) 525 6992
Email: sufiorderintl@cs.com
Website: www.sufiorder.org

ASSEMBLY

[1] Hazrat Inayat Khan, Esoteric Papers.

[2] Hazrat Inayat Khan, The Message Volumes/ [9] The Unity of Religious Ideals/ The God Ideal/ The Personality of God.

[3] Hazrat Inayat Khan, The Message Volumes/ [9] The Unity of Religious Ideals/ The God Ideal/ Two Points of View.

[4] Hazrat Inayat Khan, The Message Volumes/ [9] The Unity of Religious Ideals/ The God Ideal/ The Personality of God.

[5] Hazrat Inayat Khan, Social and Religious Gathekas/ Religious Gathekas/ Belief and Disbelief in God.

[6] Hazrat Inayat Khan, The Message Volumes/ [6] The Alchemy of Happiness/ Stages on the Path to Self-Realization.

[7] Muhyiuddin Ibn 'Arabi, *The Wisdom of the Prophets (Fusus al-Hikam)* (Aldsworth, U.K.: Beshara Publications, 1975), 16.

[8] Ibid., 8.

[9] Cf. William C. Chittick, *The Sufi Path of Love: The Spiritual Teachings of Rumi* (Albany, N.Y.: State University of New York Press, 1983), 69.

[10] Ibid., 197.

[11] Ibid., 6.

[12] Ibid., 67.

[13] Hazrat Inayat Khan, Esoteric Papers/ Sangatha I.

[14] Cf. Louis Massignon, *La passion de Husayn ibn Mansur Hallaj, martyr mystique de l'Islam, executé à Bagdad le 26 mars 922* (Paris: Éditions Gallimard, 1975), 3:115.

[15] Fariduddin 'Attar, *Livre des Secrets (Asrar-Nama)* (Paris: Les Deux Océans, 1985), 82.

[16] Cf. William C. Chittick, *The Sufi Path of Knowledge* (Albany, N.Y.: State University of New York Press, 1989), 225.

[17] Cf. Ibn Arabi, trans. Michel Vaslan, *Etudes Traditionelles,* (May 1952): 127.

[18] Muhammad ibn 'Abdi'l-Jabbar al-Niffari, *The Mawaqif and Mukhatabat of Muhammad ibn 'Abdi'l-Jabbar al-Niffari, with Other Fragments* (London: Luzac & Co., 1935), 174.

[19] Muhyiuddin Ibn 'Arabi, *Journey to the Lord of Power: A Sufi Manual on Retreat,* trans. Rabia Terris Harris (New York: Traditions International Ltd., 1981), 63.

[20] Hazrat Inayat Khan, Volumes/ The Mysticism of Sound and Music/ Music/ Music.

[21] Hazrat Inayat Khan, The Sayings of Hazrat Inayat Kahn/ Aphorisms.

[22] Massignon, *La passion de Husayn ibn Mansur Hallaj*, 56.

[23] al-Niffari, *Mawaqif and Mukhatabat*, 90.

[24] Cf. Ibn Arabi, trans. Michel Vaslan, *Etudes Traditionelles,* (September 1949): 257.

[25] Ibid., 254.

[26] Nuruddin 'Abdurrahman Jami, *Lawa'ih: A Treatise on Sufism* (London: Royal Asiatic Society, 1914), 15.

[27] Cf. Ibn Arabi, trans. Michel Vaslan, *Etudes Traditionelles*: 261.

[28] Chittick, *Sufi Path of Knowledge*, 225–28.

[29] 'Abdul Karim al-Jili, *Universal Man* (Sherborne, U.K.: Beshara Publications, 1983), 33.

[30] Massignon, *La passion de Husayn ibn Mansur Hallaj,* 72.

[31] Chittick, *Sufi Path of Knowledge*, 105.

[32] Jami, *Lawa'ih*, 28.

[33] 'Attar, *Livre des secrets*, 51.

[34] Cf. Arthur J. Arberry, *Sufism: An Account of the Mystics of Islam* (London: Unwin Paperbacks, 1979), 52.

[35] *Abu Bakr Muhammad al-Kalabadhi, The Doctrine of the Sufis (Kitab al-Ta'arruf li-madhhab ahl al-tasawwuf)* (1935; reprint, Cambridge: Cambridge University Press, 1977), 94.

[36] Reynold A. Nicholson, *The Mystics of Islam* (1914; reprint, New York: Schocken Books, 1975), 59.

[37] Annemarie Schimmel, *Mystical Dimensions of Islam* (Chapel Hill, N.C.: University of North Carolina Press, 1975), 331.

[38] Nuruddin 'Abdurrahman Jami, *Les jaillissements de lumière: Lavayeh* (Paris: Les Deux Océans, 1982), 109.

[39] Hazrat Inayat Khan, The Sayings of Hazrat Inayat Kahn/ Vadan/ Ragas.

[40] Schimmel, *Mystical Dimensions of Islam*, 364.

[41] Massignon, *La passion de Husayn ibn Mansur Hallaj,* 179.

[42] Jami, *Lawa'ih*, 125.

[43] Hazrat Inayat Khan, Healing, the Mind World, Chapter ix.

[44] Hazrat Inayat Khan, Supplementary Papers/ Philosophy, & Knowledge of Truth.

[45] Chittick, *Sufi Path of Knowledge*, 225.

[46] Ibn 'Arabi, *Wisdom of the Prophets*, 63.

[47] Fariduddin 'Attar, *The Conference of the Birds: Mantiq ut-tair* (Berkeley: Shambhala Publications, 1971), 31.

[48] Ibn 'Arabi, *Wisdom of the Prophets*, 15.

[49] al-Jili, *Universal Man*, 5.

[50] Ibid., 31.

[51] Hazrat Inayat Khan, The Sayings of Hazrat Inayat Khan/ Gayan/ Boulas.

[52] Hazrat Inayat Khan, Esoteric Papers/ Sangitha I.

[53] Hazrat Inayat Khan: The Message Volumes/ [12] The Vision of God and Man/ The Sufi Ideal.

LIGHT

[1] Hazrat Inayat Khan, Esoteric Papers/ Sangatha.

[2] Cf. Chittick, *Sufi Path of Knowledge*, 217.

[3] Hazrat Inayat Khan, Esoteric Papers.

[4] Cf. Henry Corbin, *The Man of Light in Iranian Sufism,* trans. Nancy Pearson. (Boulder and London: Shambhala Publications, 1978; New Lebanon, N.Y.: Omega Publications Inc., 1994), 23.

[5] Hazrat Inayat Khan, Spiritual Liberty/ Metaphysics/ The Destiny of the Soul/ Self-Realization.

[6] Hazrat Inayat Khan, The Soul Whence and Whither.

[7] Hazrat Inayat Khan, Spiritual Liberty Manifestation.

[8] Hazrat Inayat Khan, Esoteric Papers/ Sangathas III.

[9] Hazrat Inayat Khan, Esoteric Papers/ Sangithas ii.

[10] Hazrat Inayat Khan, The Smiling Forehead/ Sufi Teachings.

[11] Hazrat Inayat Khan, Pearls from the Ocean Unseen/ Kaza and Kadr.

[12] Corbin, *Man of Light*, 74.

[13] Ibid.

[14] Hazrat Inayat Khan, The Unity of Religious Ideals/ Prophets and Religions, The Symbol of the Sun.

[15] Hazrat Inayat Khan, Healing and the Mind World/ Mental Purification/ Insight.

[16] Hazrat Inayat Khan, Esoteric Papers/ Githa III/ Insight/ Vision (2).

[17] Maulana Jalal al-Din Rumi, *Rumi, Poet and Mystic, 1207–1273: Selections from His Writings,* trans. Reynold A. Nicholson (London: G. Allen and Unwin, 1950), 125.

[18] Cf. Henry Corbin, *Spiritual Body and Celestial Earth: From Mazdean Iran to Shi'ite Iran*, trans. Nancy Pearson (Princeton, N.J.: Princeton University Press, 1977), 134.

[19] Cf. Corbin, *Spiritual Body and Celestial Earth,* 125.

[20] Ibid., 124.

[21] Ibn Arabi, trans. Michel Vaslan, Etudes Traditionelles.

[22] Fariduddin 'Attar, *Le Livre de l'Épreuve (Musibatnama)* (Paris: Librairie Arthème Fayard, 1990), 70.

[23] Ibid., 69.

[24] Hazrat Inayat Khan, The Smiling Forehead/ Sufi Teachings.

[25] Cf. Chittick, *Sufi Path of Knowledge*, 218.

[26] Cf. Corbin, *Man of Light*, 73.

[27] Cf. Corbin, *Spritual Body and Celestial Earth,* 226.

[28] Chittick, *Sufi Path of Knowledge*, 226.

[29] Ibid., 215.

[30] Ibid., 225.

[31] Hazrat Inayat Khan, Smiling Forehead.

[32] Hazrat Inayat Khan, Philosophy Psychology, and Mysticism.

[33] Ibid.

[34] Ibid.

[35] Cf. Chittick, *Sufi Path of Knowledge*, 218–19.

[36] Henry Corbin, *L'imagination créatrice dans le Soufisme d'Ibn 'Arabi*. (1958; reprint; Paris: Flammarion, 1975), 61.

[37] Ibid., 187.

[38] Ibid., 147.

[39] 'Attar, *Livre des Secrets*.

[40] Ibid.

[41] Cf. Mehmed Ali Aini and F.J. Simore-Munir, *Un grand saint de l'Islam, Abd-al-Kadir Guilani (1077 – 1166)*. (Paris: Librairie Orientaliste Paul Geuthner, 1938) 187.

[42] Ibn 'Arabi, *Journey to the Lord of Power*, 36.

[43] Hazrat Inayat Khan, Social Gathekas/ The Awakening of the Soul.

[44] Hazrat Inayat Khan, Social Gathekas.

[45] Hazrat Inayat Khan, In an Eastern Rosegarden.

[46] Hazrat Inayat Khan, The Mind World/ Health.

[47] Hazrat Inayat Khan, The Soul Whence and Whither?; The purpose of Life.

[48] Hazrat Inayat Khan, The Mysticism of Sound and Music/ The Power of the Word/ Cosmic Language.

[49] Hazrat Inayat Khan, Esoteric Papers/ Sangathas III.

[50] Mahmud Shabistari, *Gulshan i raz: The Mystic Rose Garen of Sa'd du din Mahmud Shabistari*, trans. E. H. Whinfield (London: Trübner & Co., 1880), 15.

[51] Ibn Arabi, trans. Michel Vaslan, "Oraisons Metaphysiqu," *Etudes Traditionelles*.

[52] Maulana Jalaluddin Rumi, *Open Secret: Versions of Rumi*, trans. John Moyne and Coleman Barks, 1984), 50.

[53] Reynold A. Nicholson, *The Mystics of Islam* (1914; reprint, New York: Schocken Books, 1975), 59.

[54] Ibn Arabi, trans. Michel Vaslan, *Etudes Traditionelles*, (1961) 144.

[55] Ibn Arabi, trans. Michel Vaslan, "Oraisons Metaphysiqus," *Etudes Traditionelles*.

[56] Corbin, Man of Light, 17.

[57] Corbin, *Spiritual Body and Celestial Earth*, 124.

[58] Ibn Arabi, trans. Michel Vaslan, *Etudes Traditionelles*, (March 1949): 87.

[59] Corbin, *Spiritual Body and Celestial Earth*, 103.

[60] Hazrat Inayat Khan, Philosophy/ Psychology and Mysticism (Spirit Within and Without).

[61] Hazrat Inayat Khan, Esoteric Papers/ Githa.

[62] Hazrat Inayat Khan, Esoteric Papers/ Githa III.

[63] Ibid.

[64] Corbin, *Spiritual Body and Celestial Earth*, 123.

[65] Ibid., 132.

[66] Mahmud Shabistari, *The Secret Rose Garden of Sa'd du Din Mahmud Shabistari*, trans. Florence Lederer (Grand Rapids, Mich.: Phanes Press, 1987), 80.

[67] Ibn Arabi, trans. Michel Vaslan, *Etudes Traditionelles* (1952): 132.

[68] Cf. Corbin, *Spiritual Body and Celestial Earth*, 124.

[69] Hazrat Inayat Khan, Aqibat/ Life After Death/ Manifestation (2).

[70] Hazrat Inayat Khan, Spiritual Liberty/ Metaphysics/ Our Constitution.

[71] Hazrat Inayat Khan, The Mysticism of Sound and Music/ The Power of the Word.

[72] Hazrat Inayat Khan, Philosophy/ Psychology, Mysticism, Spirit and Matter.

[73] Hazrat Inayat Khan, Gatha II/ Superstitions, Customs, and Beliefs/ The Greek Mysteries.

[74] Hazrat Inayat Khan, The Alchemy of Happiness/ The Continuity of Life.

[75] Hazrat Inayat Khan, Esoteric Papers.

[76] Cf. Chittick, *Sufi Path of Knowledge*, 124.

[77] Corbin, *Spiritual Body and Celestial Earth*, 219.

[78] Ibid., 180.

[79] Eric John Holmyard, *Alchemy* (New York: Penuin Books, 1979).

[80] Ibid.

ASCETICISM

[1] Rumi, *Essential Rumi*.

[2] Shamsuddin Muhammad Hafiz, *I Heard God Laughing* (Walnut Creek, Calif.: Sufism Reoriented, 1996), 13.

[3] Rumi, *Essential Rumi*.

[4] Hafiz, *I Heard God Laughing*, 9.

[5] Ibid., 99.

[6] Hazrat Inayat Khan, The Message Volume/ [3] The Art of Personality.

[7] Hazrat Inayat Khan, The Sayings of Hazrat Inayat Khan/ Bowl of Saki.

[8] Hazrat Inayat Khan, Esoteric Papers/ Githa I/ The Path of Attainment/ Attitude.

[9] Hazrat Inayat Khan, Volumes/ [5] Spiritual Liberty/ Interest and Indifference.

[10] Fariduddin Attar, *Muslim Saints and Mystics: Episodes from the Tadhkirat al-Auliyaj,* trans. A. J. Arberry (London: Routledge & Kegan Paul, 1966), 43–44.

[11] Hazrat Inayat Khan, Gayan/ Boulas.

[12] Hazrat Inayat Khan, Esoteric Papers/ Sangitha I.

[13] Hazrat Inayat Khan, Social and Religious Gathekas/ Social Gathekas/ Happiness.

[14] Hazrat Inayat Khan, The Message Volumes/ [7] In an Eastern Rose Garden/ The Freedom of the Soul (2).

[15] Maulana Jalaluddin Rumi, *Divani Shamsi Tabriz* (San Francisco: The Rainbow Bridge, 1973), 112.

[16] Schimmel, *Mystical Dimensions of Islam,* 323.

[17] Hazrat Inayat Khan, Social and Religious Gathekas/ Social Gathekas/ Renunciation.

[18] Hazrat Inayat Khan, The Sayings of Hazrat Inayat Khan/ Gayan/ Chalas.

[19] Hazrat Inayat Khan, The Sayings of Hazrat Inayat Khan/ Aphorisms.

[20] Hazrat Inayat Khan, Esoteric Papers/ Gatha III/ Symbology/ Layla and Majnun.

[21] Rumi, *Essential Rumi,* 6–7.

[22] Hafiz, *I Heard God Laughing,* 15.

[23] ‘Abdul Qadir al-Jilani (Gilani), *Utterances of Shaikh ‘Abd al-Qadir al-Jilani (Malfuzat),* trans. Muhtar Holland (Houston, Tex.: Al-Baz Publishing, 1992), 128.

[24] Ibid., Schimmel, *Mystical Dimensions of Islam,* 364.

[25] al-Jilani, *Utterances,* 94–96.

[26] Hazrat Inayat Khan, Social Gathekas.

[27] Khaliq Ahmad Nizami, *The Life and Times of Shaikh Farid-u’d-din Ganj-i-Shakar* (Aligarh, India: Muslim University, 1955), 51.

[28] Abu ’Ali Ibn Sina (Avicenna), *Avicenne, Le récit de Hayy ibn Yaqzan* (Tehran: Commission des Monuments Nationaux de l’Iran, 1953), 18.

[29] Ibid., 55.

[30] Hazrat Inayat Khan, The Sayings of Hazrat Inayat Khan/ Aphorisms.

[31] Hazrat Inayat Khan, The Message Volumes/ [8] Sufi Teachings/ The Privilege of Being Human/ Self Realization.

[32] Reynold A. Nicholson, *Studies in Islamic Mysticism* (Cambridge and New York: Cambridge University Press, 1978), 49.

[33] Ibid., 55.

[34] Cf. Chittick, *Sufi Path of Knowledge,* 157–59.

[35] Hazrat Inayat Khan, Social and Religious Gathekas/ Social Gathekas/ The Problem of The Day: Home and Reform.

[36] Hazrat Inayat Khan, Esoteric Papers/ Sangtha I.

[37] Hazrat Inayat Khan, The Message Volumes/ [3] The Art of Personality/ Education/ The Education of the Infant.

[38] al-Jilani, *Utterances,* 41.

[39] Hazrat Inayat Khan, The Message Volumes/ [6] The Alchemy of Happiness/ Interest and Indifference.

[40] Hazrat Inayat Khan, Esoteric Papers.

[41] Hazrat Inayat Khan, Esoteric Papers/ Sangtha III.

[42] Hazrat Inayat Khan, The Message Volumes/ [1] The Way of Illumination.

[43] Hazrat Inayat Khan, The Message Volumes/ [6] The Alchemy of Happiness/ Reaction.

[44] Hazrat Inayat Khan, The Message Volumes/ [22] The Mysticism of Sound and Music/ Cosmic Language/ The Ego.

[45] Hazrat Inayat Khan, Esoteric Papers/ Gathas.

[46] Hazrat Inayat Khan, The Path of Initation.

[47] Hazrat Inayat Khan, The Purpose of Life.

[48] Hazrat Inayat Khan, The Soul Whence and Whither.

[49] Hazrat Inayat Khan, Volumes/ [6] The Alchemy of Happiness/ The Development of Personality.

[50] Hazrat Inayat Khan, Volumes/ [8] Sufi Teachings/ The Privilege of Being Human/ Sacrifice.

[51] Hazrat Inayat Khan, Esoteric Papers/ Githa I.

[52] Hazrat Inayat Khan, The Path of Initiation.

[53] Hazrat Inayat Khan, Cosmic Language.

[54] Hazrat Inayat Khan, Alchemy.

[55] Hazrat Inayat Khan, Philsophy, Psychology, and Mysticism.

[56] Hazrat Inayat Khan, Alchemy.

[57] Cf. William C. Chittick, *The Sufi Doctrine of Rumi: An Introduction* (Tehran: Aryamehr University, 1974), 43.

[58] Hazrat Inayat Khan, The Supplementary Papers/ Psychology/ Psychology V/ The Story of the Hyderbad Sage.

[59] Hazrat Inayat Khan, The Message Volumes/ [9] The Unity of Religious Ideals/ The Message and the Messenger.

[60] Chittick, *Sufi Doctrine of Rumi,* 53.

[61] Shabistari, *Gulshan i raz,* 15.

[62] Ibid., 16.

[63] Ibid., 7.

[64] Ibid., 17.

[65] Hazrat Inayat Khan, Volumes/ [12] The Vision of God and Man/ Mastery (1).

[66] Cf. Chittick, *Sufi Path of Love,* 69.

[67] Hazrat Inayat Khan, The Message Volumes/ [11] Philosophy, Psychology, Mysticism/ Mysticism in Life/ Mysticism in Life.

[68] Hazrat Inayat Khan, The Inner Life/ The Object of the Journey.

[69] Quoted by Hazrat Inayat Khan from memory in Philosophy, Psychology and Mysticism.

[70] Cf. Nicholson, *Mystics of Islam*, 115.

[71] Hazrat Inayat Khan, Gayan.

[72] Hazrat Inayat Khan, Religious Gathekas.

[73] Hazrat Inayat Khan, Gayan.

[74] Hazrat Inayat Khan, The Way of Illumination; Private Papers.

[75] Hazrat Inayat Khan, Gathekas 17/ Sufi Mysticism III: Preparing the Heart for the Path of Love.

[76] Hazrat Inayat Khan, Cosmic Language.

BASTAMI

[1] R. C. Zaehner, *Hindu and Muslim Mysticism* (London: The Athlone Press, University of London; New York: Oxford University Press, 1960), 203.

[2] Carl W. Ernst, *Words of Ecstasy in Sufism* (Albany, N.Y.: State University of New York Press, 1985), 30.

[3] Hazrat Inayat Khan, The Message Volumes/ [14] The Smiling Forehead/ Pairs of Opposites Used in Religious Terms.

[4] Zaehner, *Hindu and Muslim Mysticism*, 95.

[5] Cf. Louis Massignon and Paul Kraus, *Akhbar al-Hallaj: Texte ancien relatif à la prédication et au supplice du mystique musulman al-Hosseyn B. Mansour al-Hallaj* (Paris: Éditions Larose, 1936), 55.

[6] Ibid., 62.

[7] Hazrat Inayat Khan, Philosophy, Psychology, and Mysticism.

[8] al-Kalabadhi, *Doctrine of the Sufis* , 15.

[9] Ali ibn Uthmanal-Hujwiri. *The Kashf al-Mahjub, the Oldest Persian Treatise on Sufism* (London: Luzac & Co., 1911) 367–69.

[10] Cf. Zaehner, *Hindu and Muslim Mysticism*, 54.

[11] al-Jili, *Universal Man*, 113.

[12] Zaehner, *Hindu and Muslim Mysticism*, 113.

[13] Muhyiuddin Ibn 'Arabi, *"Whoso Knoweth Himself…" from the Treatise on Being (Risale-t-ul-wujudiyyah)* (London: Beshara Publications, 1976), 6–9.

[14] Jami, *jaillissements de lumière*, 117.

[15] Husayn ibn Mansur al-Hallaj, *The Tawasin of Mansur al-Hallaj: The Great Sufic Text on the Unity of Reality* (Berkeley and London: Diwan Press, 1974), 42.

[16] Cf. Massignon, *La passion de Husayn ibn Mansur Hallaj*, 1:530.

[17] Cf. Henry Corbin, *L'imagination créatrice dans le Soufisme d'Ibn 'Arabi* (Paris: Flammarion, 1975), 65.

[18] al-Jili, *Universal Man*, 3.

[19] Jami, *jaillissements de lumière*, 85.

[20] Ibid., 99.

[21] Ibid., 97.

[22] Louis Gardet, *Expérience mystique en terre non-chrétienne* (Paris: Alsatia, 1954), 135–57.

[23] Cf. Schimmel, *Mystical Dimensions of Islam*, 306

[24] Cf. Zaehner, *Hindu and Muslim Mysticism*, 199–206.

[25] Ibid., 201–8.

[26] Ibid., 221.

[27] Ibid., 218–19.

[28] Hazrat Inayat Khan, The Message Volumes/ [8] Sufi Teachings/ Privilege of Being Human/ Self-Realization.

[29] Cf. Ibn Arabi, trans. Michel Vaslan, *Etudes Traditionelles*, (September 1949): 258.

[30] Zaehner, *Hindu and Muslim Mysticism*, 222.

[31] Jami, *Lawa'ih*, 10.

[32] Hazrat Inayat Khan, The Message Volumes/ [1] The Way of Illumination; The Inner Life; The Soul Whence and Whither?; The Purpose of Life/ The Way of Illumination/ Some Aspects of Sufism/ Some Esoteric Terms.

[33] Hazrat Inayat Khan, The Message Volumes/ Spiritual Liberty/ Aqibat, Life After Death/ Manifestation (1).

[34] Hazrat Inayat Khan, The Message Volumes/ [6] the Alchemy of Happiness/ The Aim of Life.

[35] Cf. Zaehner, *Hindu and Muslim Mysticism*, 208–9.

[36] Hazrat Inayat Khan, The Way of Illumination.

[37] Martin Lings, *A Moslem Saint of the Twentieth Century: Shaikh Ahmad al-'Alawi* (London: George Allen & Unwin Ltd, 1961), 127.

[38] Cf. Zaehner, *Hindu and Muslim Mysticism*, 198–99.

[39] Ibid., 200.

[40] Ibid., 206.

[41] Ibid., 207.

[42] Ibid., 219.

[43] Cf. Henry Corbin, *Creative Imagination in the Sufism of Ibn 'Arabi* (London: Routledge & Keagan Paul Ltd., 1970), 191.

[44] Ibid., 114.

[45] Zaehner, *Hindu and Muslim Mysticism*, 207.

[46] Seyyed Hossein Nasr, *Three Muslim Sages: Avicenna, Shurawardi and Ibn'Arabi* (New York: Caravan Books, 1976), 9.

[47] Cf. Zaehner, *Hindu and Muslim Mysticism,*
198–99.

[48] Ibid., 205–6.

[49] Cf. Ernst, *Words of Ecstasy in Sufism,* 26.

[50] Zaehner, *Hindu and Muslim Mysticism,* 223.

[51] Cf. Massignon, *La passion de Husayn ibn Mansur
Hallaj,* 3:53.

[52] Ibid., 114–15.

[53] Ibid., 116.

[54] Ibid., 115.

[55] Ibid., 116.

[56] Hazrat Inayat Khan, The Message Volumes/ [9]
The Unity of Religious Ideals/ The Message and
the Messenger.

[57] Hazrat Inayat Khan, Esoteric Papers/ Githa II/
Meditation/ The Purpose of Life.

[58] Hazrat Inayat Khan, The Message Volumes/ [8]
Sufi Teachings/ Privilege of Being Human/
Spirituality.

[59] Hazrat Inayat Khan, The Message Volumes/ [9]
The Unity of Religious Ideals/ the God Ideal/
Three Steps.

[60] Hazrat Inayat Khan, Esoteric Papers/ Gatha I/
Morals/ The Jarring Effect of the Ego of Another.

[61] Hazrat Inayat Khan, Spiritual Liberty.

[62] Hazrat Inayat Khan, The Message Volumes/ [12]
The Vision of God and Man/ Confessions:
Autobiographical Essays of Hazrat Inayat Khan/
My interest in Sufism.

[63] Ibid.

[64] Hazrat Inayat Khan, The Message Volumes/ [4]
Healing and the Mind World/ Mental Purification/
Mastery.

[65] Hazrat Inayat Khan, The Message Volumes/ [7]
In an Eastern Rose Garden/ Will Power.

[66] Cf. Corbin, *Creative Imagination,* 123–25.

[67] Ibid., 125.

[68] Cf. Nicholson, *Studies in Islamic Mysticism,* 1.

[69] R. S. Bhatnagar, *Dimensions of Classical Sufi
Thought* (London: East-West Publications, 1984),
61.

[70] Cf. Corbin, *Creative Imagination,* 129.

[71] Cf. Corbin, *L'imagination créatrice,* 16.

[72] Cf. Chittick, *Sufi Path of Knowledge,* 290.

[73] Hazrat Inayat Khan, Mind World.

[74] Hazrat Inayat Khan, Volumes/ [6].

CREATIVITY

[1] Hazrat Inayat Khan, The Message Volumes/ [2]
The Mysticism of Sound and Music/ Cosmic
Language/ The Ego.

[2] Chittick, *Sufi Path of Knowledge,* 297.

[3] Nicholson, *Mystics of Islam,* 80–81.

[4] Hazrat Inayat Khan, The Supplementary Papers/
Philosophy/ Philosophy III/ Illusion and Reality.

[5] Hazrat Inayat Khan, The Message Volumes/ [5]
Spiritual Liberty/ Aqibat, Life After Death/ The
Philosophy of the Soul.

[6] Hazrat Inayat Khan, Private Papers.

[7] Hazrat Inayat Khan, The Message Volumes/ [5]
Spiritual Liberty/ Metaphysics/ The Experience of
the Soul/ The Experience of the Soul through the
Spirit.

[8] Chittick, *Sufi Path of Knowledge,* 351–52.

[9] Hazrat Inayat Khan, The Message Volumes/ [8]
Sufi Teachings/ Health and Order of Body and
Mind/ Dreams/ Dreams Are of Three Kinds.

[10] Hazrat Inayat Khan, Esoteric Papers/ Sangatha ll.

[11] Hazrat Inayat Khan, The Message Volumes/ [5]
Spiritual Liberty/ Metaphysics/ The Experience of
the Soul/ The Experience of the Soul Through the
Spirit.

[12] Hazrat Inayat Khan, The Message Volumes/ [5]
Spiritual Liberty/ Aqibat, Life After Death/ The
Philosophy of the Soul.

[13] Kevin Shepherd, *A Sufi Matriarch: Hazrat
Babajan* (Cambridge: Anthropographia
Publications, 1985), 55.

[14] Cf, Corbin, *Man of Light,* 69.

[15] Cf. Ibn Arabi, trans. Michel Vaslan, *Etudes
Traditionelles,* (April–May 1952): 129.

[16] Shabistari, *La roseraie du mystère,* 406.

[17] Chittick, *Sufi Path of Knowledge,* 406.

[18] Ibid., 87.

[19] Hazrat Inayat Khan, The Messages Volumes/ [4]
Healing and the Mind World/ Mental Purification/
Mastery.

[20] Cf. Corbin, *Spiritual Body and Celestial Earth,*
127.

[21] Hazrat Inayat Khan, The Message Volumes/ [5]
Spiritual Liberty/ Aqibat, Life After Death/ The
Philosophy of the Soul.

[22] Hazrat Inayat Khan, The Message Volumes/ [11]
Philosophy, Psychology, Mysticism/ Mysticism in
Life/ The Visions of the Mystic.

[23] Cf. Ibn Arabi, trans. Michel Vaslan, *Etudes
Traditionelles,* (June 1952): 183.

[24] Hazrat Inayat Khan, The Message Volumes/ [4]
Healing and the Mind World/ Mental Purification/
The Control of the Mind.

[25] Hazrat Inayat Khan, The Soul, Whence and
Whither?/ Toward Manifestation.

[26] Hazrat Inayat Khan, The Message Volumes/ [4]
Healing and the Mind World/ The Mind World/
Chapter XI.

[27] Hazrat Inayat Khan, The Message Volumes/ [11]
Philosophy, Psychology, Mysticism/ Mysticism in
Life/ Mysticism in Life.

[28] Ibid.

[29] Quoted by Hazrat Inayat Khan.

[30] Hazrat Inayat Khan, The Message Volumes/ [1]
The Way of Illumination; the Inner Life; the Soul/
Whence and Whither?; the Purpose of Life/ The
Soul, Whence and Whither?/ Manifestation.

[31] Hazrat Inayat Khan, The Message Volumes/ [6]
The Alchemy of Happiness/ The Aim of Life.

[32] Hazrat Inayat Khan, The Message Volumes/ [6]
The Alchemy of Happiness/ Man, the Master of
His Destiny.

[33] Hazrat Inayat Khan, Social Gathekas.

[34] Hazrat Inayat Khan, Esoteric Papers/ Sangatha
II.

[35] Ibn 'Arabi, *Wisdom of the Prophets*, 24.

[36] Jami, *jaillissements de lumière*, 143.

[37] Corbin, *Man of Light*, 106.

[38] Rumi, *Essential Rumi.*

[39] Rumi, *Essential Rumi.*

[40] Corbin, *Creative Imagination*, 214.

[41] Cf. Ibn Arabi, trans. Michel Vaslan, *Etudes
Traditionelles* (July–Ocotober 1961): 248.

[42] Hazrat Inayat Khan, The Message Volumes/ [2]
The Mysticism of Sound and Music/ Cosmic
Language/ The Form of Thought.

[43] Corbin, *Creative Imagination.* 197.

[44] Chittick, *Sufi Path of Knowledge*, 354.

[45] Hazrat Inayat Khan, The Message Volumes/ [1]
The Way of Illumination; the Inner Life; the Soul
Whence and Whither?; the Purpose of Life/ The
Soul, Whence and Whither?/ Manifestation.

[46] Hazrat Inayat Khan, The Message Volumes/ [2]
The Mysticism of Sound and Music/ The
Mysticism of Sound/ Form.

[47] Corbin, *Spiritual Body and Celestial Earth*, 219.

[48] Shepherd, *Sufi Matriarch.*

[49] Quoted by Hazrat Inayat Khan, Sufi Teachings.

[50] Nizamuddin Auliya, *Nizam ad-din Awliya, Morals
for the Heart: Conversations of Shaykh Nizam ad-
din Awliya recorded by Amir Hasan Sijzi* (New
York: Paulist Press, 1992), 253.

RUMI

[1] Cf. Chittick, *Sufi Path of Love*, 302.

[2] Rumi, *Divani Shamsi Tabriz*, 31.

[3] Ibid., 85.

[4] Chittick, *Sufi Path of Love,* 141.

[5] Ibid., 263.

[6] Ibid., 342–43.

[7] Schimmel, *Mystical Dimensions of Islam*, 191.

[8] Cf. Chittick, *Sufi Path of Love*, 264–65.

[9] Maulana Jalaluddin Rumi, *Teachings of Rumi: The
Masnavi* (New York: E. P. Dutton & Co., 1975), 3.

[10] Chittick, *Sufi Path of Love*, 263.

[11] Ibid., 297.

[12] Ibid., 263.

[13] Ibid., 343.

[14] Ibid., 219.

[15] Ibid., 285.

[16] Ibid., 169.

[17] Ibid., 168.

[18] Ibid., 298.

[19] Awliya, *Nizam ad-din*, 67.

[20] Chittick, *Sufi Path of Love*, 263.

[21] Ibid., 267.

[22] Ibid., 304.

[23] Ibid., 302–4.

[24] Ibid., 335.

[25] Ibid., 267.

[26] Ibid., 298.

[27] Ibid., 203.

[28] Ibid., 197.

[29] Hazrat Inayat Khan, Volumes/ [5] Spiritual
Liberty/ Love, Human and Divine/ The
Philosophy of Love.

[30] Hazrat Inayat Khan, Volumes/ [6] The Alchemy
of Happiness/ The Purpose of Life (1).

[31] Hazrat Inayat Khan, Volumes/ [11] Philosophy,
Psychology, Mysticism/ Mysticism in Life/ Beauty.

[32] Chittick, *Sufi Path of Love*, 215.

[33] Corbin, *Creative Imagination*, 146.

[34] Jami, *jaillissements de lumière*, 53.

[35] Ibid., 103.

[36] Hazrat Inayat Khan, Volumes/ [2] The Mysticism
of Sound and Music/ Music/ Music.

[37] Cf. Chittick, *Sufi Path of Love*, 320.

[38] Ibid., 339.

[39] Ibid., 313.

[40] Ibid., 312.

[41] Chittick, *Sufi Path of Love*, 344.

[42] Ibid., 307.

[43] Hazrat Inayat Khan, Addresses to Cherags.

[44] Hazrat Inayat Khan, Class for Mureeds.

[45] Cf. Corbin, *l'imagination créatice.*

[46] Shabistari, *Secret Rose Garden*, 87–88.

[47] Margaret Smith, *Rabia the Mystic: Her Fellow-
Saints in Islam* (Cambridge and New York:
Cambridge University Press, 1928), 102.

TRANSCEND

[1] Corbin, *Creative Imagination,* 133.

[2] al-Niffari, *Mawaqif and Mukhatabat,* 50.

[3] Ibn 'Arabi, *Wisdom of the Prophets,* 15.

[4] Ibid., 23.

[5] Ibid., 36.

[6] Ibn 'Arabi, *Les Illuminations de la Mecque/The Meccan Illuminations/Al-Futuhat al-Makkiyya,* trans. Michel Chodkiewicz (Paris: Éditions Sinbad,1988), 362.

[7] Hazrat Inayat Khan, The Message Volumes/ [5] Spiritual Liberty/ A Sufi Message of Spiritual Liberty/ Self-Knowledge.

[8] Ibn 'Arabi, *Wisdom of the Prophets,* 16.

[9] Ibid., 12.

[10] Ibid., 14.

[11] al-Niffari, *Mawaqif and Mukhatabat,* 64.

[13] al-Jili, *Universal Man,* 19.

[14] Ali ibn Uthman al-Hujwiri, *The Kashf al-Mahjub, the Oldest Persian Treatise on Sufism* (London: Luzac & Co., 1911), 269–70.

[15] al-Jili, *Universal Man,* 31.

[16] Ibn Arabi, trans. Michel Vaslan, *Etudes Traditionelles,* (December 1948): 343.

[17] Chittick, *Sufi Path of Knowledge,* 298.

[18] Ibid., 231.

[19] Corbin, *Creative Imagination,* 197.

[20] Cf. Ibid.

[21] Corbin, *Creative Imagination,* 174.

[22] al-Niffari, *Mawaqif and Mukhatabat,* 30.

[23] Chittick, *Sufi Path of Knowledge,* 298.

[24] Ibid., 297.

[25] Ibid., 41.

[26] Ibn 'Arabi, *"Whoso Knoweth Himself…",* 4.

[27] Reynold A. Nicholson, *A Literary History of the Arabs.* (1907; reprint, Cambridge: Cambridge University Press, 1941), 336.

[28] Ibn Arabi, trans. Michel Vaslan, *Etudes Traditionelles* (April 1952): 27.

[29] Ibn Arabi, trans. Michel Vaslan, "La Station de la Futuwwah et ses secrets, chapter 146 of Futuhat al-Makkya," *Etudes Traditionelles:* 19.

[30] al-Kalabadhi, *Doctrine of the Sufis,* 48.

[31] Husayn ibn Mansur al-Hallaj, *Diwan* (Paris: Éditions du Seuil, 1981), 50.

[32] Massignon, *Passion of al-Hallaj,* 3:62–63.

[33] Jami, *jaillissements de lumière,* 113.

[34] Massignon, *Passion of al-Hallaj,* 3:128.

[35] Ibid., 127.

[36] al-Jili, *Universal Man,* 32.

[37] Chittick, *Sufi Path of Knowledge,* 131–32.

[38] Ibn 'Arabi, *Wisdom of the Prophets,* 42, 57.

[39] Arthur J. Arberry, *Avicenna on Theology* (London: John Murray, 1951), 35.

[40] Ibn Arabi, trans. Michel Vaslan, *Etudes Traditionelles,* (April–May 1952): 131.

[41] Ibn 'Arabi, *"Whoso Knoweth Himself…",* 16.

[42] Massignon, *Passion of al-Hallaj,* 3:319.

[43] Ibn 'Arabi, trans. Michel Vaslan, *Etudes Traditionelles,* (April–May 1952): 131.

[44] al-Niffari, *Mawaqif and Mukhatabat,* 28.

[45] Chittick, *Sufi Path of Knowledge,* 228.

[46] Ibid., 225.

[47] Ibn Arabi, trans. Michel Vaslan, *Etudes Traditionelles,* (1984).

[48] Cf. Ibn Arabi, trans. Michel Vaslan, *Etudes Traditionelles,* (July–October): 248.

[49] Muhyiuddin Ibn 'Arabi, *La parure des Abdal (Hilyatu-l-Abdal)* (Paris: Les Éditions de l'Oeuvre, 1992), 21.

[50] al-Niffari, *Mawaqif and Mukhatabat.*

[51] Hazrat Inayat Khan, The Message Volumes/ [9] The Unity of Religious Ideals/ The God Ideal/ The Existence of God.

[52] Hazrat Inayat Khan, Healing.

[53] Hazrat Inayat Khan, The Message Volumes/ [14] The Smiling Forehead/ Sufi Teachings.

[54] Hazrat Inayat Khan, Social and Religious Gathkas/ Social Gathekas/ The Awakening of the Soul.

[55] Hazrat Inayat Khan, The Message Volumes/ [14] The Smiling Forehead/ Sufi Teachings.

[56] Ibn 'Arabi, *Illuminations de la Mecque,* 361.

[57] Hazrat Inayat Khan, The Message Volumes/ [6] The Alchemy of Happiness/ Purity of Life.

[58] Hazrat Inayat Khan, The Sayings of Hazarat Inayat Khan/ Aphorisms.

[59] Ibn 'Arabi, *Journey to the Lord of Power,* 35.

[60] Hazrat Inayat Khan, The Message Volumes/ [4] Healing and the Mind World/ Mental Purification/ The Distinction Between Subtle and Gross.

[61] Hazrat Inayat Khan, Social and Religious Gathekas/ Social Gathekas/ The Awakening of the Soul.

[62] Hazrat Inayat Khan, Esoteric Papers/ Gatha I/ Insight/ Divine Evidence.

HALLAJ

[1] Massignon, *La passion de Husayn ibn Mansur Hallaj,* 3:50–51.

[2] Ibid., 55.

[3] Ibn Arabi, trans. Michel Vaslan, *Etudes Traditionelles,* (September, 1949): 262.

[4] Massignon, *La passion de Husayn ibn Mansur Hallaj,* 3:50.

[5] al-Hallaj, *Diwan,* 133.

[6] Massignon, *La passion de Husayn ibn Mansur Hallaj,* 3:72.

[7] Ibid., 50.

[8] Hazrat Inayat Khan, The Sayings of Hazrat Inayat Khan/ Gayan/ Suras.

[9] Zaehner, *Hindu and Muslim Mysticism,* 137.

[10] Massignon, *La passion de Husayn ibn Mansur Hallaj,* 3:53.

[11] Seyyed Hossein Nasr, ed., *Islamic Spirituality: Manifestations* (New York: The Crossroad Publishing Company, 1991), 148.

[12] Shabistari, *roseraie du mystère,* 42–43.

[13] al-Jilani. *Utterances,* 94.

[14] Lings, *Moslem Saint of the Twentieth Century,* 197.

[15] Ibid., 198.

[16] Chittick, *Sufi Path of Knowledge.*

[17] Shabistari, *roseraie du mystère,* 28.

[18] Cf. Rumi, *Rumi, Poet and Mystic.*

[19] Cf. Corbin, *Man of Light,* 88.

[20] Cf. Massignon and Kraus, *Akhbar al-Hallaj,* 6.

[21] Ibid., 47.

[22] Al-Hallaj, *Diwan,* 113.

[23] Ibn Arabi, trans. Michel Vaslan, *Etudes Traditionelles,* (September 1949): 261.

[24] Chittick, *Sufi Path of Love,* 191.

[25] Ibid., 192.

[26] Ibid., 193.

[27] Ibn Arabi, trans. Michel Vaslan, *Etudes Traditionelles,* (September 1949): 258.

[28] 'Abdullah-i Ansari, *Munajat: The Intimate Prayers* (New York: Khaneghah and Maktab of Maleknia Naseralishah, 1975), 75.

[29] Cf. Massignon, *Passion of al-Hallaj,* 99.

[30] Henry Corbin, *Suhrawardi d'Alep, fondateur de la doctrine illuminative (ishraqi)* (Paris: G. P. Maisonneuve, 1939), 31.

[31] Chittick, *The Sufi Doctrine of Rumi,* 31.

[32] Ibn Arabi, trans. Michel Vaslan, *Etudes Traditionelles,* (December 1948): 343.

[33] Cf. Corbin, *Suhrawardi d'Alep,* 31.

[34] Ibn 'Arabi, "Whoso Knoweth Himself…", 21.

[35] Ernst, *Words of Ecstasy in Sufism,* 29.

[36] al-Jili, *Universal Man,* 14.

[37] Ibn Arabi, trans. Michel Vaslan, *Etudes Traditionelles,* (September 1949): 251.

[38] Massignon, *Passion of al-Hallaj,* 475.

[39] Massignon, *Passion de Husayn ibn Mansur Hallj,* 2:280.

[40] al-Jilani, *Utterances,* 94.

[41] Massignon and Kraus, *Akhbar al-Hallaj,* 72.

[42] Hazrat Inayat Khan, The Sayings of Hazrat Inayat Khan/ Vadan/ Alankaras.

[43] Hazrat Inayat Khan, Esoteric Papers/ Sangatha I.

[44] Massignon, *Passion of al-Hallaj,* 596.

[45] Massignon, *Passion de Husayn ibn Mansur Hallj,* 3:79.

[46] Jami, *Lawa'ith.*

[47] Zaehner, *Hindu and Muslim Mysticism,* 139–40.

[48] Ibid., 219.

[49] Massignon, *Passion of al-Hallaj,* 3:44.

[50] Massignon, *Passion of al-Hallaj,* 1:14–15.

[51] Rumi, *Divani Shamsi Tabriz,* 88.

[52] Muslihuddin Sa'di, *Gulistan, ou Le jardin des roses* (Paris: Éditions Robert Laffont, 1980).

[53] Massignon, *Passion of al-Hallaj,* 94.

[54] al-Kalabadhi, *Doctrine of the Sufis,* 78.

[55] Massignon, *Passion of al-Hallaj,* 1:16.

[56] al-Hallaj, *Diwan,* 71.

[57] Ibid., 600.

[58] Massignon, *Passion of al-Hallaj,* 1:16.

[59] Massignon, *La passion de Husayn ibn Mansur Hallaj,* 1:57.

[60] Massignon, *Passion of al-Hallaj,* 1:17.

[61] Abu Hamid al-Ghazzali, *Mishkat al-Anwar (The Niche for Light),* trans. W.H.T. Gairdner (Lahore, India: Sh. Muhammad Ashraf, Kashmiri Bazar, 1952), 17.

[62] Ibid., 1.

[63] Ernst, *Words of Ecstasy in Sufism,* 78.

[64] Eva de Vitray-Meyerovitch, *Anthologie du soufisme* (Paris: Éditions Sindbad, 1978), 119.

[65] Massignon, *Passion of al-Hallaj,* 1:17.

[66] Ibid.

GLORIFICATION

[1] Ibn Arabi, trans. Michel Vaslan, *Etudes Traditionelles,* (September, 1949): 261.

[2] Hazrat Inayat Khan, Social and Religious Gathekas/ Religious Gathekas/ The Manner of Prayer.

[3] Arberry, *Avicenna on Theology,* 55–57.

[4] Hazrat Inayat Khan, Social and Religious Gathekas/ Religious Gathekas/ Belief and Disbelief in God.

[5] Hazrat Inayat Khan, The Message Volumes/ [1] The Way of Illumination; the Inner Life; the Soul Whence and Whither?; the Purpose of Life/ Inner Life/ The Object of the Journey.

[6] Cf. Reynold A. Nicholson, *Rumi, Poet and Mystic.* (1950; reprint, London: George Allen & Unwin, 1964), 34.

[7] Cf. Ibn Arabi, trans. Michel Vaslan, *Etudes Traditionelles,* (September 1949): 263.

[8] Hazrat Inayat Khan, The Message Volumes/ [5] Spiritual Liberty/ Aqibat, Life After Death/ Manifestation (1).

[9] Nicholson, *Studies in Islamic Mysticism,* 59.

[10] Cf. Nicholson. *Rumi, Poet and Mystic,* (reprint 1964), 173.

[11] Cf. Ernst, *Words of Ecstasy in Sufism,* 91.

[12] Ibid.

[13] Hazrat Inayat Khan, Esoteric Papers/ Gatha III/ Reason Is Earth-Born.

[14] Hazrat Inayat Khan, Social and Religious Gathekas/ Religious Gathekas/ Buddha.

[15] Hazrat Inayat Khan, The Message Volumes/ [10] The Path of Initiation/ Sufi Mysticism/ The Mystic.

[16] Hazrat Inayat Khan, The Message Volumes/ [7] In an Eastern Rose Garden/ The Four Paths Which Lead to The Goal.

[17] Bikrama Jit Hasrat, *Dara Shikuh: Life and Works* (New Delhi: Munshiram Manoharlal Publishers Pvt. Ltd., 1979), 216–20.

[18] Hazrat Inayat Khan, The Message Volumes/ [12] The Vision of God and Man/ The Vision of God and Man (2).

[19] Shabistari, *Secret Rose Garden,* 78.

[20] Kabir, *The Kabir Book: Forty-Four of the Ecstatic Poems of Kabir* (Boston: Beacon Press, 1977), 33.

[21] Ibid., 2.

[22] Moses Maimonides, *The Guide of the Perplexed,* trans. Shlomo Pines. (Chicago: The University of Chicago Press, 1963).

[23] Hazrat Inayat Khan, Smiling Forehead.

[24] Hazrat Inayat Khan, The Message Volumes/ [5] Spiritual Liberty/ A Sufi Message of Spiritual Liberty/ Prophets.

[25] Hazrat Inayat Khan, Gathekas/ Gatheka 5/ Different Schools of Sufism/ The Sufi Message.

[26] Hazrat Inayat Khan, The Way of llumination.

[27] Cf. Corbin, *Creative Imagination,* 197.

[28] Cf. Nicholson, *Rumi, Poet and Mystic,* (reprint 1964), 177.

[29] Rumi, *Divani Shamsi Tabriz,* 79.

[30] Ibid., 80.

[31] Hafiz, *I Heard God Laughing,* 27.

[32] Schimmel, *Mystical Dimensions of Islam,* 271.

[33] Hazrat Inayat Khan, Addresses to Cherags/ A New Form.

[34] Hazrat Inayat Khan, Gathekas/ Gatheka 29 Our Sacred Task: The Message.

[35] Hazrat Inayat Khan, The Message Volumes/ [9] The Unity of Religious Ideals/ The Message and the Messenger/ The Sufi Message.

THE GALAXIES

[1] Cf. Corbin, *Spiritual Body and Celestial Earth,* 123–34.

[2] Cf. Ibid., 125.

[3] Cf. Henry Corbin, *Oeuvres Philosophiques et Mystiques de Shihabaddin Yahya Sohrawardi (Opera metaphysica et mystica II)* (Tehran: Institut Franco-Iranien; Paris: Adrien-Maisonneuve, 1952), 1:56.

[4] Cf. Reynold A. Nicholson, *Rumi, Poet and Mystic.* (reprint 1964), 171.

[5] Ibid., 79.

[6] Ibid., 166.

[7] al-Hallaj, *Diwan,* 67.

[8] Cf. Corbin, *Oeuvres Philosophiques,* 1:98.

[9] Ibid., 88.

[10] Cf. Corbin, *Spiritual Body and Celestial Earth,* 125.

[11] Cf. Corbin, *Suhrawardi d'Alep,* 162.

[12] Corbin, *Spiritual Body and Celestial Earth,* 118.

[13] Cf. Nicholson, *Rumi, Poet and Mystic* (reprint, 1964).

[14] Ibid., 11.

[15] Rumi, *Divani Shamsi Tabriz,* 40.

[16] Cf. Nicholson. *Rumi, Poet and Mystic* (reprint 1964), 69.

[17] Corbin, *Oeuvres Philosophiques,* 1:39.

[18] Cf. Nicholson. *Rumi, Poet and Mystic* (reprint 1964), 42.

[19] Hazrat Inayat Khan, Volumes/ [11] Philosophy, Psychology, Mysticism/ Philosophy/ Intelligence.

[20] Hazrat Inayat Khan, Volumes/ [14] The Smiling Forehead/ Sufi Teaching.

[21] Hazrat Inayat Khan, Esoteric Papers/ Sangatha I.

[22] Hazrat Inayat Khan, Spiritual Liberty.

[23] Hazrat Inayat Khan, The Sayings of Hazrat Inayat Khan/ Aphorisms.

[24] Hazrat Inayat Khan, Volumes/ [1] The Way of Illumination; the Inner Life; the Soul Whence and Whither; the Purpose of Life.

[25] Hazrat Inayat Khan, The Sayings of Hazrat Inayat Khan/ Aphorisms.

Glossary

Alast, Day of: the primordial day when God asked the soul, "Am I not Your Lord?" And the soul replied, "Yes," sealing the covenant.

Dargah: royal court; the tomb of a saint.

Dhikr: remembrance of God; the invocation of the profession of faith, *"La ilaha illa'llah"* (There is no God but God).

Fravarti: angelic counterpart; soul.

Ghaus ul-A'zam: the "Great Reliever"; epithet of Shaykh 'Abd ul-Qadir Jilani.

Hadith: a saying traditionally held to be an authentic statement of the Prophet.

Hadith qudsi: a saying traditionally held to be an authentic statement of God proffered by the Prophet.

Haqq: the truth; God.

Houris: nymphs of paradise.

Hurakhsh, Prince: the angel of the Sun.

Hurqalya: the heavens of the 'Alam ul-Mithal, the World of the Image.

Iblis: the fallen archangel who was banished from heaven for having refused to obey God by recognizing God in man (in view of the unity of being).

Imam: prayer leader

Jabalqa and Jabarsa: two fabled cities in Hurqalya.

Ka'bah: the cubical shrine at Mecca, of axial sanctity, housing the Black Stone, its foundation traced to Abraham.

Khadim: one who serves; custodian of a saint's tomb.

Khorasan: a Central Asian province, situated in contemporary northeastern Iran and western Afghanistan.

Khwaja: lord; title of respect for a sage.

La ilaha illa'llah: "There is no God but God": *nothing exists apart from the Divine Being.*

Maya: a Hindu concept purporting that things are illusory, deceptive—the physical world is not the way it appears, our problems are not what we assess them to be, our self-image is not whom we are.

Murshid: "Guide," Sufi teacher.

Pir: "Elder," Sufi teacher.

Pir-o-murshid: "Elder and Guide," Sufi teacher.

Pre-eternity: infinity prior to created time.

The Prophet (ar-Rasul): Muhammad (peace and blessings be upon him)

Qur'an Sharif: "The Noble Qur'an," the scripture revealed by God to the Prophet Muhammad, consisting of 114 Surahs (chapters).

Tawhid: unification.

Ibn Adham—Ibrahim ibn Adham (d. 790) was known as the prince who renounced his kingdom of Balkh for the most extreme asceticism and poverty, though he took menial jobs to earn a living. He considered that renunciation of the goods of the world is only valid if it is paired with renunciation of oneself by practicing anonymity. He carried this to the extreme by putting up with the most abject dejection and humiliation.

Ahsa'i—Ahmad Ahsa'i (1753–1826) had dreams of the twelve Imams in his youth, which prompted him to study theology and to travel to the holy cities of Najaf and Karbala to train. After he was certified, he went to Iran and worked as an itinerant teacher for fifteen years. His work involved exploring the process of the resurrection of the body as an alchemical operation.

'Alawi—Shaykh Ahmad 'Alawi (b. 1869) of Mostaganem, Algeria, was described in his late years as a noble, serene, and exceptional human being of spiritual magnitude. His teachings may serve as a clue to awakening in life: While perceiving the sensory world, one can use the signs in which God reveals Him/Herself as catalysts to trigger off what ibn 'Arabi calls "our supra-sensory perception."

Hazrat 'Ali—Hazrat 'Ali ('Ali b. Abi Talib) was the first Imam in the Shiite Branch of Islam, and figures at the top of most of the chains authenticating an apostolic succession in Sufism. This is true of the Sunni Branch as well, because it is related that the Prophet assigned him the task of ensuring the esoteric tradition to several groups. He was the first in the order of the esoteric masters who follow the beginning of prophecy.

Ansari—Shaykh 'Abdullah Ansari (1006-89), whose tomb is venerated in Herat, Afghanistan, is known for his description of the stages followed by those advancing on the spiritual path in the book *Manazil us Sa'irin.* According to the Sufis, adepts pass through different phases or stations, and Ansari made a very sensitive study of the sequence, thus outlining a kind of topography of inner states that might serve as guidelines to the adept.

Ibn 'Arabi—Muhyi ud-Din Ibn 'Arabi (1165-1240) is often surnamed Shaykh ul-Akbar (the great Shaykh). He left detailed instructions for novices and adepts following the Sufic ascetic discipline. Although he referred to his "investiture" by Khidr (the Muslim equivalent of Elijah) in the desert, the spiritual preceptor who introduced him into the ways of the Sufis was a lady: Fatima of Cordova.

Ibn 'Ata—Ibn 'Ata (Abu'l-Abbas Sahl Amuli Adami), proved himself a staunch friend and supporter of Hallaj. Ibn 'Ata was the only disciple of Hallaj who stood up for him at his trial and was executed 14 days before Hallaj. He vituperated against his accusers on the jury for the ruthless taxation of the poor and the corruption of the political authorities in power. They responded with blows and threw him to the gallows.

'Attar—Fariduddin 'Attar (1142–1220), celebrated as one of Iran's most prestigious poets, conveyed his admiration for the Sufis by writing a biography of the better known Sufi mystics: the *Tadhkirat ul-Auliya,* that became a classic. In a subsequent book, *Misibat Namah,* he revealed himself to be Sufi mystic, and in a later book reflected on the preparation for resurrection and the ascent of the soul in worlds of light.

Ibn Sina—Abu 'Ali Husayn Ibn Sina, (b. 980) (also known as Avicenna), is known as a Muslim philosopher of rare genius who also influenced the Christian scholastics. He gained some renown for his famous *Canon of Medicine* and his involvement in some state functions.

Aristotle's Metaphysics was a springboard from which he explored a new outlook on cosmology. His works express, by way of symbols, spiritual discoveries in the realm of metaphor.

Hazrat Babajan—Gul-rukh (rose faced) (d. 1931) was the scholarly and aristocratic descendant of a princely family of the Pathan dynasty in Afghanistan. She escaped from home on her wedding day at eighteen and found a teacher in Rawalpindi (now in Pakistan). In her later years she lived in a poor area of Poona, India in a makeshift shack under a Neem tree. There were rumors of healing and miraculous powers.

Baqli—Ruzbihan Baqli (b. 1128) experienced a spiritual "unveiling" that prompted him to forsake his vegetable shop (Baqli means "the greengrocer") to wander and enter a Sufi novitiate. He was initiated in Pasa and wandered again, eventually settling in Shiraz. In Mecca he is reported (by Ibn 'Arabi, no less) to have fallen in love with a singing girl. This episode may have inspired his later work, *The Jasmine of Lovers,* which explores the subtle interplay between human and divine love.

Bastami—Abu Yazid Tayfur Bastami, (sometimes spelled Bistami, otherwise known as Bayazid Bistami) (d. 874), of Zoroastrian origin, was an austere ascetic and wanderer of the arid mountains and deserts of northern Iran. His proclamation: "O! I" and "How great is my glory," sound even more explicit than the "I am the Truth" of Hallaj. Bastami escaped the scaffold because his critics considered him to be insane, lost in divine ecstasy.

Hajji Bektash—Hajji Bektash, born in Eastern Iran, founded the Bektashi Sufi Order, of dervishes, the most liberal of all Sufi Orders. Women participate fully in meetings and practices, and the order does not forbid drinking wine. They hold that human love can lead to divine love by being transfigured in the ascent of the human soul. Welcoming spiritual centers of this order are still to be found in Turkey and even in Bulgaria.

Dara Shikuh—Prince Dara Shikuh (1615–1659), son of Shah Jahan and Mumtaz Mahal, heir apparent to the throne of the Mogul kings of India, tried to demonstrate in his work, *Majma' ul-Bahrayn,* the similarities between Hinduism and Islam. Taking advantage of the accusations of heresy by the orthodox, his younger brother Aurangzeb, who coveted the throne, killed him and imprisoned their father Shah Jehan.

Ibn Da'ud—Ibn Da'ud (d. 909) was the judge who condemned Hallaj to be tortured, crucified, and incinerated. He was an implacable jurist who believed Hallaj was an infidel who did not obey Islamic law: that he was satanic, an antichrist. Da'ud implemented his verdict in a juridical indictment which was a judicial interpretation of the Qur'an.

Emre—Yunus Emre was an illiterate blacksmith who, owing to his wit and authenticity, won many hearts, particularly in Turkey, with his highly evocative poetry in the popular Turkish style. His poetry reflected the spiritual aspirations of his people, spirited by ecstasy and without the pedantry of theologians.

Farsi—Salman Pak Farsi, was a Christian convert wandering in the desert when he was captured and enslaved by the tribes. The Prophet heard of his plight, raised the funds to free him, and gave him the status of a member of the Prophet's family. Farsi ranked second after the Prophet among the *"ahl us-suffa,"* a small group of initiates who met on the "sofa" in a hall opposite the Mosque of Medina, and established the basis of esotericism of Islam.

Ganj-i Shakar—Shaykh Farid Ganj-i Shakar (1175–1265) was the second-in-line successor of Khwaja Mu'in ud-Din Chishti. Ganj-i Shakar was blessed both by him and by Khwaja Qutub ud-din Bakhtiyar Kaki—a rare occurrence in the history of Sufism. When he left Delhi to avoid disagreement over Chishti policy and went to live in a mud hut in the Pakistani Punjab, he was so popular that a sizeable portion of the population of Delhi followed him there.

Ghazali—Abu Hamid Ghazali (b. 1059), was known for a book in which he refuted the contentions of philosophers as "mind trips" devoid of experiential foundation. At the age of 36, he left his office as professor of philosophy at the Baghdad University and renounced his family. Living as a Sufi pilgrim, he visited Damascus, Jerusalem, Alexandria, Mecca, and Medina. Then, suddenly, he returned to the teaching profession, a transformed being.

Gilani—'Abd ul-Qadir Gilani (1088–1161), who is traditionally given the title Ghauth ul-'Azam (a high rank in the spiritual hierarchy), was an example of the blending of power and humility. His condemnation of sensual and carnal desires may sound judgmental to our modern ears, but this approach gives a clue to the secret of spiritual power, which he considered a saving grace against the abuses of secular power.

Hafiz—Muhammad Shams ud-Din Hafiz (b. 1388), is popularly known as Hafiz (the one who knows the Qur'an by heart). A beloved Iranian court poet who made no claim to being a Sufi, he defied religious authorities when he exposed the hypocrisy, even masochism, of the puritans. He was accused of Epicureanism and ostracized by most of the Sultans of his time, except for the Indian Abu Ishaq.

Hallaj—Mansur Hallaj (the martyr of Islam) (b. 857) was rejected for his views by his then spiritual guide, Junayd Baghdadi, who predicted his end on the gallows. Hallaj was in conflict with the religious authorities of his time because he encouraged personal sanctification rather than submission to authority. He was tried in Baghdad and crucified. For him death was the annihilation of the self in the ultimate union with the divine Beloved.

Hamadani—'Ayn ul-Qudat Hamadani (1098–1131) was already charged with heresy by age fourteen. He went on to become a brilliant scholar, and was inspired by Ghazali. He was accused of holding pantheistic views that were in conflict with Junayd's views on divine transcendence. He was convicted, imprisoned, and put to death at age 33.

Hujwiri—Abu'l-Hasan ibn Uthman 'Ali Hujwiri (1009–1072) (also called Data Ganj Bakhsh), whose tomb is in Lahore, was the first Sufi to establish a large following in India. His encounter with Hindu ascetics may well have influenced him in favoring sobriety over euphoria (ecstasy), which sets the tone of his famous work *Kashf ul-Mahjub* (the rendering of the veil), a concise treatise on Sufism.

Jami—Maulana 'Abd ur-Rahman Jami, who won the admiration of astronomers by solving their problems, is best known for his large collection of biographies of Sufis and his mystical masterpiece *Lawa'ih,* which contrived to reconcile contradictory theological views by highlighting the live experience of Sufi mystics. Jami saw human love as a step toward divine love, since love demands the renunciation of the personal ego.

Jili—'Abd ul-Karim Jili (b. 1366, d. 1408–1417) was an erudite scholar of Sufi doctrine, and also seemed gifted with personal experience of the states he described. His metaphysics were based upon the gigantic worldview of Ibn 'Arabi, although he differed on certain points. Jili brings into perspective the archetypes of man called the universal man, the title of his famous book.

Junayd—Abu'l-Qasim Junayd of Baghdad (d. 909) had a widespread influence in Islamic mysticism. He highlighted the divine transcendence, condemning as pantheistic any view referring to God as immanent. He condemned ecstasy, (i.e. in Bastami), and advocated sobriety instead. He condemned Hallaj for valuing that which is gained by the existential state.

Kabir—Kabir was the champion of Muslim-Hindu unity in a divided society. His abrasive yet humorous criticism of both Hindus and Muslims popular superstitions was so irritating to both groups, that his own Pir (Sufi preceptor), Shaykh Taqqi, arraigned him before Emperor Sikander Lodi. His escape from a death sentence could well be attributed to his disarming wit.

Azar Kayvan—Azar Kayvan was a native of Istakhar, the seat of the ancient kings from whom he traced his descent. His early years were spent in seclusion, receiving guidance in dreams from the mystic philosophers of Greece, India, and Iran. In later life he settled in Patna, India, where under Akbar Shah's liberal policy he presided over a universalist esoteric school. His poetry describes cosmic initiations, encounters with archangelic intelligences, and ecstasies of *unio mystica.*

Kalabadhi—Abu Bakr Muhammad Kalabadhi (d. 990) of Bukhara is known for his book *Kitab ut-Ta'arruf* in which he endeavored to demonstrate the orthodoxy of Sufi doctrines from the point of view of Islam. In this book, Kalabadhi enumerated eminent Sufis, described their tenets, and the steps in the spiritual journey, and defines the consecrated terms used by Sufis.

Kharraz—Abu Sa'id Bakr (born 'Isa Kharraz) (d. 890) anticipated Hallaj by declaring only God has the right to say "I." He taught that when man become annihilated from his attributes, he attains to perfect subsistence, and fostered the representation by the contemplative of the image of God

which sets the pace for prayer as a dialogue. As a result of these teachings, he was condemned and banished.

Abi'l-Khayr—Abu Sa'id ibn Abi'l-Khayr (965-1049) up to the age of 40, subjected himself to the most drastic mortification, including a retreat of 40 days suspended upside down in a well repeating the dhikr. During those years he said he found it difficult to talk to people, but to God: Ah! At age forty, he suddenly changed from an anchorite to a convivial host who exacted large sums from the wealthy by performing miracles to provide feasts for the poor.

Khidr—Khidr, (called the "Naqib ul-Aulia," the warden of the saints) is often looked upon as the Islamic counterpart of Elijah. A quasi-legendary figure, he was described by travelers lost or thirsting in the desert as the "green man of the desert" (therefore called al khadir), who comes to the rescue of the forlorn. He was also invoked by a number of Sufis as their disincarnate spiritual guide in the "other world" or realm of metaphor or mystery.

Hazrat Inyat Khan—Hazrat Inayat Khan (1891–1927) was proclaimed a prestigious musician by the Nizam of Hyderabad when he was still a young man. He was named as the spiritual successor of Khwaja Abu Hashim Madani and told to take the message of Sufism to the West. He established Sufi centers in most European countries and the United States. His teaching was based on experience rather than dogma. He called it the Message of spiritual freedom.

Pir Vilayat Inayat Khan—Pir Vilayat Inayat Khan (1916–) is the spiritual head of the Sufi Order International and the successor of his father Hazrat Pir o Murshid Inayat Khan of the Chishti Sufi Order. He has a MA in Psychology and is a scholar in comparative religion and a veteran meditation teacher. He is exploring ways of meditation that deal with the problems and way of thinking of our day, and is in dialogue with other religious practitioners, as well as with physicists, biologists, and psychotherapists.

Khusrau—Amir Khusrau (b.1253) was known in India as a poet of versatile genius, He was a prime disciple and venerated friend of Khwaja Nizam ud-Din. While a staunch Sufi, he was free from prejudices, and laughed at pedantic scholars, hypocritical would-be Sufis, gullible bigots, and the snobbery of aristocrats. He could laugh, sing, and dance and enjoy even the rather worldly entertainment of the Palace, including wine and dancing girls.

Kubra—Najm ud-Din Kubra (1145–1221) (who was killed in the mogul invasion) sought to find the light of the macrocosm in our own light as microcosm. Visions of light, grasped by senses beyond our faculties of sense perception, can give us clues to the condition of our soul. He found that the way to avoid succumbing to the flaw of courting vision for self-aggrandizement was by purifying oneself by concentrating on God

Ni'matullah—Shah Ni'matullahi (1331–1431) founder of the most prominent Sufi Order in Iran, escaped in his travels from an encounter with Tamerlane and then settled in Kirman. He taught awakening in life, service to fellow beings, and kindness in a spirit of kinship. He set an example for his followers by working as a farmer while constantly recollecting God. He did not advocate retirement from the world, though he disapproved of ostentation.

Madani—Sayyid Abu Hashim Madani (d. 1907) was the teacher of Hazrat Inayat Khan, whose own succession was from Sayyid Hasan Jili Kalimi. He studied law as a young man and was known as a distinguished scholar and mystic, but lead a quiet and inconspicuous life in the Purana Pul Quarter of Hyderabad.

Maimonides—Abraham Maimonides (1186–1237), son of the Jewish philosopher Moses Maimonides, was a leading figure in the Jewish Diaspora. Like other Jews fleeing the persecution of the crusades, he was inspired by Sufi ascetics. He was initiated in a Sufi Order, but little is known of the Jewish Sufi pietist movement that flourished in Egypt in the thirteenth century, whose adepts called themselves *Khassidims,* pious.

Majriti—Maslamah Majriti's life and mystical vision is wrapped in mystery since it emerged out of the secret doctrine of the Sabeans. They were a syncretistic hermetic sect which aimed at reconciling religious sects. They were permeated by Neo-Platonism and inspired by the hermetic gnosis linked with Jabir ibn Hayyan's esoteric alchemy and the advent of Ismaelism.

Mu'in ud-Din Chishti—Khwaja Mu'in ud-Din Chishti (b. 1142) was so successful in revealing Sufism to the predominantly Hindu population of India, that the Raja of Ajmer attempted to banish him. The Raja was thwarted when the city was placed under siege by the troops of a sultan. This event was ascribed to the Khwaja's miraculous powers. His mausoleum in Ajmer is the focal point of masses of pilgrims, including devotees of all religions.

Naqshband—Baha ud-Din Naqshband preached strict adherence to Islamic law. He advocated asceticism to counteract the selfishness and hypocrisy of worldliness, but preferred purification to mortification. His asceticism did not lead to estrangement from the world, but to God-consciousness in the midst of everyday activities. His practice of *dhikr* was silent and internal, and he eschewed the audition and whirling of dervishes.

Niffari—'Abd ul-Jabbar Niffari (d. 965) was a little-known wandering dervish from the precincts of ancient Babylon, who was intoxicated by his rapture in the revelations which he said he received from God. His ecstatic pronouncements, culled during his occasional visits to his son-in-law's home and probably noted down by his daughter, were most likely elaborated into manuscripts under the titles *Mawaqif* and *Mukhataba*.

Nizam ud-Din — Khwaja Nizam ud-Din (d. 1325), despite poverty, received a good religious education. After gaining a reputation has a formidable scholar, he renounced his career and became a disciple of Khwaja Farid ud-Din, whom he eventually succeeded. In Delhi he presided over a Sufi hospice where princes mingled with paupers. The village of Basti Hazrat Nizamuddin has grown around his tomb.

Dhu'n-Nun — Dhu'n-Nun was the surname given to Thauban Ibn Ibrahim Misri, (d. 859). It was said he was an alchemist, had deciphered the hieroglyphs, and had magical powers. Yet his personality was meek and humble, and his poetry reveals a being moved by the ecstasy of divine love. He was the first to introduce the spiritual audition, to define the spiritual stages of the adept, and to point out the difference between acquired knowledge and revealed knowledge.

Baba Kuhi — Baba Kuhi was considered as a mad man because he was so absorbed in God that he was totally out of touch with the world. His tomb, near Shiraz, has been a traditional place of pilgrimage. Today it attracts Iranian hippies playing Rock and Roll, but in the basement you will find many photographs of earlier very dignified and austere Sufi dervishes who bear the demeanor of the kings of ancient law.

Rabi'a — Rabi'a 'Adawiyya (717-810) is held with great reverence among the Sufis. She has remained through the centuries in the minds of the Sufis the epitome of unconditional love, discarding offers of marriage for the way of the ascetic. She was concerned that her love of

God should be totally disinterested. She was particularly wary lest her acts of devotion should find a reward in the Qur'anic promise of a lovely afterlife in paradise.

Rumi — Maulana Jalal ud-Din Rumi (1207-1273) was the son of a respected Muslim theologian who fled the hordes of Ghengis Khan in 1220. On the way the 7-year-old child was blessed by Farid-ud-Din Attar, who predicted that he would become a great Sufi poet. By 1244 Rumi was a university professor, when he met Shams-ud-Din Tabriz. Tabriz asked him a question so disturbing, that Rumi left his career and was transformed into a Sufi mystic.

Sa'di — Muslih ud-Din Sa'di, of Shiraz (d 1292), Iran's romantic troubadour of love, was a nonconformist free-minded hedonist. As a young man fleeing the devastation wreaked by the hordes of Ghengis Khan, he wandered, an insatiable traveler far and wide in the desert caravans destitute and starving. In his books he intimates that he still seeks solitude in quest of the wisdom of the art of living with fervor.

Sahl Tustari — Sahl ibn 'Abdullah Tustari, (d. 896) the mentor of Hallaj in his early days, inspired a community of dervishes in Abadan, then Basra. He demonstrated a combination of religious zeal (trust in God) and repentance, together with earning a living in the world. He respected the religious Islamic law, while voicing views that were questionable for the religious authorities, which resulted in his exile to Basra.

Shabistari — Sa'id ud-Din Mahmud Shabistari (1250–1320), became famous for his book *The Rose Garden of Mystery,* which was both popular in his time and inspired generations of Sufis. Reading it today in the light of the holistic paradigm in physics, one cannot but be amazed. He describes man as a microcosm that manifests the bounty of that macrocosm that is the universe

Shams of Tabriz—Shams ud-Din Muhammad ibn 'Ali Malik of Tabriz is known as the one who unlocked the muse of poetry in Maulana Jalal ud-Din Rumi, but little else is known about him. From descriptions, he was handsome, impressive, radiant, majestic and regal, and gifted with a natural authority. Arrogantly defiant of officialdom, he did not suffer fools gladly.

Shibli—Abu Bakr Shibli (d. 945) testified against Hallaj at his trial. On the way to the gallows, Hallaj borrowed Shibli's prayer rug. The prayers completed, the passersby threw stones at Hallaj; Shibli threw a rose. Hallaj sighed and said, "The rose of the friend is more painful than the stones of the enemies." At one point Shibli was interred in an asylum, and he said that he had declared the same views as Mansur, but his insanity saved his life.

Shushtari—Abu'l-Hasan Shushtari (d. 1269) was an itinerant mendicant and poet from Cadiz in Andalusia, and the foremost disciple of Ibn Sab'in, the Aristotelian mystic known for his answers to the questions of emperor Frederick II Hohenstaufen. In addition to his highly acclaimed *diwan*, Shushtari composed prose works which elaborate the Sab'inian tradition, which traces its esoteric genealogy to Hermes.

Simnani—Abu'l-Makarim Rukn ud-Din 'Ala' ud-Daulah Simnani (b. 1261–1336), an aristocrat, served at the court as a young man until a series of visionary experiences prompted him to immerse himself in penitence and study under the guidance of a shaykh of Baghdad. He left a corpus of Arabic and Persian writings that has proven highly influential, within his own Kubrawi order and beyond.

Suhrawardi—Shihab ud-Din Yahya Suhrawardi (b. 1191) aimed to restore the universal illuminative tradition which was founded upon a communion with the archangels of the spheres. Sohrawardi considered himself to be the successor of Hermes, Buzurgmehr, Kay Khusrau, Frashaostra (the latter three Zoroastrian magi), Pythagoras, and Plotinus.

'Uways Qarani—'Uways Qarani lived in Yemen and never met the Prophet, yet he was devoted to him. The Prophet is said to have described 'Uways and said that 'Uways would interceded for many of the Prophet's people at the time of the resurrection. 'Uways represents for the Muslims the prototype of all those who are dedicated to the Prophet without having known him, that is, the overwhelming masses of the faithful.

Zib un-Nisa—Princess Zib un-Nisa (1639–1689) was the eldest daughter of the puritanical Mughal emperor Aurangzib. She ventured to write a commentary *(tafsir)* on the Qur'an—which she had memorized at age seven—but was prevented by her father. She succeeded, however, in composing a *diwan* of soulful Persian poetry, under the nom de plume *Makhfi* ("the Hidden").

Bibliography

Fariduddin 'Attar. *The Conference of the Birds, Mantiq ut-tair.* Berkeley: Shambhala Publications, 1971.

——. *Le Livre de l'Épreuve (Musibatnama).* Translated from Persian by Isabelle de Gastines. Paris: Librairie Arthème Fayard, 1990.

Ansari, 'Abdullah-i. *Munajat, The Intimate Prayers.* Translated by Lawrence Morris and Rustam Sarfeh. New York: Khaneghah and Maktab of Maleknia Naseralishah, 1975.

Arberry, Arthur J. *Avicenna on Theology.* London: John Murray, 1951.

——. *Sufism: An Account of the Mystics of Islam.* London: Unwin Paperbacks, 1979.

Awiliya, Nizam ad-din. *Nizam ad-din Awliya, Morals for the Heart. Conversations of Nizam ad-din Awiya recorded by Amir Hasan Sijzi.* Translated and annotated by Bruce B. Lawrence. New York: Paulist Press, 1992.

Bhatnagar, R.S. *Dimensions of Classical Sufi Thought.* London and The Hague: East-West Publications, 1984.

Chittick, William C. *The Sufi Doctrine of Rumi, An Introduction.* Tehran: Aryamehr University, 1979.

——. *The Sufi Path of Love, An Anthology of Sufism.* London: Luzac & Co Ltd., 1954.

Corbin, Henry. *Creative Imagination in the Sufism of Ibn 'Arabi.* Translated by Ralph Manheim. London: Routledge & Kegan Paul Ltd., 1970.

——. *L'imagination créatrice dans le Soufisme d'Ibn 'Arabi.* Paris: Flammarion, 1975.

——. *The Man of Light in Iranian Sufism.* Translated by Nancy Pearson. Boulder and London: Shambhala Publications, 1978 and New Lebanon, N.Y.: Omega Publications Inc., 1994.

——. *Oeuvres Philosophiques et Mystiques de Shihabaddin Yahya Sohrawardi (Opera metaphysica et mystica II).* Tehran: Institute Franco-Iranien and Paris: Adrien-Maisonneuve, 1952.

——. *Suhrawardi d'Alep, fondateur de la doctrine illuminative (ishraqi).* Paris: G.P. Maisonneuve, 1939.

Ernst, Carl W. *Words of Ecstasy in Sufism.* Albany, N.Y.: State University of New York Press, 1985.

Gardet, Louis. *Expérience mystique en terre non-chrétienne.* Paris: Alsatia, 1954.

Hafiz, Shamsuddin Muhammad. *I Heard God Laughing.* Renderings of Hafiz by Daniel Ladinsky. Walnut Creek, Calif.: Sufism Reoriented, 1996.

al-Hallaj, Husayn ibn Mansur. *Diwan.* Translated from Arabic by Louis Massignon. Paris: Éditions du Seuil, 1981.

——. *The Tawasin of Mansur al-Hallaj, The Great Sufic Text on the Unity of Reality.* Translated by Aisha Abd ar-Rahman at-Tarjumana. Berkeley and London: Diwan Press, 1974.

al-Hujwiri, Ali ibn Uthman. *The Kashf al-mahjub, the Oldest Persian Treatise on Sufism.* Translated by Reynold A. Nicholson. London: Luzac & Co, 1911.

Ibn 'Arabi, Muhyiuddin. *Les Illuminations de la Mecque. The Meccan Illuminations. Al-Futuhat al-Makkiyya.* (Textes choisis/Selected Texts). Translated under the direction of Michel Chodkiewicz. Paris: Éditions Sindbad, 1988.

——. *"Who So Knoweth Himself ..." from the Treatise on Being (Risale-t-ul-wujudiyyah).* Translated from Arabic by T.H. Weir. London: Beshara Publications, 1976.

——. *The Wisdom of the Prophets (Fusus al-Hikam).* Translated from Arabic to French with notes by Titus Burckhardt. Translated from French by Angela Culme-Seymour. Aldsworth, U.K.: Beshara Publications, 1975.

——. *Etudes Traditionelles.* Translated by Michel Vaslan. (This periodical published a series of excerpts from the works of Ibn 'Arabi over a period of several years.)

Jami, Nurruddin 'Abdurrahman. *Les jaillissements de lumière. Lavayeh.* Edited and translated by Yann Richard. Paris: Les Deux Océans, 1982.

——. *Lawa'ih. A Treatise on Sufism.* Translated by E.H. Whinfield and Mirza Muhammad Kazvini. London: Royal Asiatic Society, 1914.

al-Jilani, Abdul Qadir. *Utterances of Shaikh 'Abd al-Qadir al-Jilani (Malfuzat).* Translated by Muhtar Holland. Houston, Tex.: Al-Baz Publishing Inc., 1992.

al-Jili, 'Abdul Karim. *Universal Man.* Extracts translated with commentary by Titus Burckhardt. English Translation by Angela Culme-Seymour. Sherborne, U.K.: Beshara Publications, 1983.

Kabir. *The Kabir Book. Forty-Four of the Ecstatic Poems of Kabir.* Versions by Robert Bly. Beacon Press, Boston, 1977.

al-Kalabadhi, Abu Bakr Muhammad. *The Doctrine of the Sufis (Kitab al-Ta'arruf li-madhhab ahl al-tasawwuf).* Translated from Arabic by A.J. Arberry. 1935. Reprint, Cambridge, London, and New York: Cambridge University Press, 1977.

Lings, Martin. *A Moslem Saint of the Twentieth Century, Shaikh Ahmad al-'Alawi.* London: George Allen & Unwin Ltd., 1961.

Maimonides, Moses. *The Guide of the Perplexed.* Translated by Shlomo Pines. Chicago: The University of Chicago Press, 1963.

Massignon, Louis and Paul Kraus. eds. *Akhbar al-Hallaj.* Translated by Louis Massignon and Paul Kraus. Paris: La Rose, 1936.

Massignon, Louis. *La passion de Husayn Ibn Mansur Hallaj, martyr mystique de l'Islam, executé à Bagdad le 26 mars 922.* Volumes I–IV. Paris: Éditions Gallimard,1975.

Nasr, Seyyed Hossein. *Three Muslim Sages, Avicenna – Suhrawardi – Ibn 'Arabi.* New York: Caravan Books, 1976.

Nicholson, Reynold A. *A Literary History of the Arabs.* 1907. Reprint, Cambridge: Cambridge University Press, 1941.

——. *The Mystics of Islam.* 1914. Reprint, London and Boston: Routledge and Kegan Paul, 1963 and New York: Schocken Books, 1975.

——. *Rumi, Poet and Mystic.* 1950. Reprint, London: George Allen & Unwin, 1964.

——. *Studies in Islamic Mysticism.* Cambridge, London, and New York: Cambridge University Press, 1978.

al-Niffari, Muhammad ibn 'Abdi'l-Jabbar. *The Mawaqif and Mukhatabat of Muhammad ibn 'Abdi'l-Jabbar al-Niffari, with other fragments.* Edited and translated by Arthur J. Arberry. London: Luzac & Co, 1935.

Rumi, Maulana Jalaluddin. *Open Secret, Versions of Rumi.* Translated by John Moyne and Coleman Barks. Putney, Vt.: Threshold Books, 1984.

——. *Selected poems from the Divani Shamsi Tabriz.* Cambridge: Cambridge University Press, 1898.

——. *Teachings of Rumi, The Masnavi.* Translated and abridged by E.H. Whinfield. New York: E.P.Dutton & Co Inc., 1975.

Sa'di, Muslihuddin. *Gulistan ou Le jardin des roses.* Paris: Éditions Robert Laffont, 1980.

Shabistari, Mahmud. *Gulshan i raz: The Mystic Rose Garden of Sa'd du din Mahmud Shabistari.* Translated from Persian by E.H. Whinfield. London: Trübner & Co., 1880.

——. *The Secret Rose Garden of Sa'd du Din Mahmud Shabistari.* Translated from Persian by Florence Lederer. Lahore: Sh. Muhammad Ashraf, Kashmiri Bazar, n.d. and Grand Rapids, Mich.: Phanes Press, 1987.

Shepherd, Kevin. *A Sufi Matriarch: Hazrat Babajan.* Cambridge: Anthropographia Publications, 1985.

de Vitray-Meyerovitch, Eva. *Anthologie du soufisme.* Paris: Éditions Sindbad, 1978.

Zaehner, R.C. *Hindu and Muslim Mysticism.* London: The Athlone Press, University of London and New York: Oxford University Press Inc., 1960.

Author Acknowledgments

The concept of this rather unusual book has unfurled in the course of many decades as, with ever increasing enthusiasm and amazement, I perused the wonderful books in my collection on Sufism in my library. I discovered the bounty and alacrity in the insight and in the views of the great Sufi dervishes of the past, a quality borne from the fact that these old teachers applied their spiritual attunement to real life and everyday situations in their own culture. Inspired by them, I meditated on the implication of their teachings upon my way of thinking.

These perspectives in the less known horizons of the mind, where spiritual enlightenment is carried beyond commonplace cogitations, have been studied and translated for readers during the past years by the professors of Islamic mysticism. It is thanks to their comments and interpretations on the Sufi spiritual tradition that this book became at all a possibility. I have quoted their insight and wisdom in my own book, and hence my thanks go to these scholars for inspiring *In Search of the Hidden Treasure,* and this also applies to scholars in kindred religions.

This book is basically fiction built out of an academic background in an endeavor to make Sufism more accessible to the broader public unfamiliar with the subtleties of Sufi metaphor.

In its initial stages, I was simply recording notes on my computer without any intention of their being assembled in a book. Therefore in my enthusiasm, I noted the particularly significant statements of the Sufi mystics, but did not stop at checking their references. Later, at the time that I was asked to make a book out of all this bounty, I had to spend years of tedious and time-consuming work hunting for the relevant references. Owing to my continuous scheduling of workshops, lectures, meditations, and teachings this could not be completed in time for publication, hence there are a few references missing

The reader will of course notice that I have quoted my own father Hazrat Pir-o-Murshid Inayat Khan profusely. Apart from the reverence with which I hold him, this can be accounted for by the fact that he was perhaps the very first teacher to present to his disciples in the West the views of the ancient Sufis. Hazrat Inayat Khan was responding to his disciples' need to understand what the Sufi mystics were conveying in their culture and metaphysical lore and how it could be applied in the context of the trend of thinking in modern societies, and he was thus instrumental in making their views more accessible for readers.

My own commentaries are a further effort to answer queries of those interested in Sufism, typical of many similar questions I have encountered in my seminars when trying to point out the implications of these Sufi insights in terms of everyday people's problems, concerns, and quest for personal creativity.

In Search of the Hidden Treasure has been a concerted effort on the part of an exceptional team of people who worked with me in its creation for the last two years. My deep thanks go to Joel Fotinos, the talented publisher at Tarcher/Putnam, and to my editor Mitch Horowitz who encouraged me in my vision. Philip Dunn, Manuela Dunn, and Priya Hemenway were the creative force that made my text come alive in the beautiful volume that you hold in your hands, and my deepest thanks goes to them too. Julie Foakes was the gifted and persevering art editor who tracked all the images in the book, often from obscure places and mostly involving hours, days, weeks, and months of careful research and without her talents we could not have illustrated the book with such rare and stunning art. Two gifted copy-editors worked on the text, Jonathan Kauffman and Sangeet Duchane, checking every word and reference and rechecking it all again: the text benefited immensely from your patience and skill. Finally, Victoria Pohlmann wove her magic with the layout and designed the book beautifully, making it something to treasure for all who will buy it. My son Pir Zia Inayat Khan helped me with the manuscript and I am proud of the legacy that has been passed on to him and of the wisdom he embodies. Devi Tide, of the Sufi Order, has coordinated between all the different people and teams and my gratitude goes out to her too.

There are certain individuals who have helped and inspired me over the years, and my thanks is extended to them also: Mariel Walters, Telema Hess, Dorothy Craig, Raqib Ickovits, Michael David Clarkson, Sharif Graham, Amida Cary, Yasodhara Sandra Lillydahl, Musawwira Butta, and Kerubiel Inayat Khan, who have helped edit the manuscript. I also particularly wish to thank Jyoti Jessica Roshan and Melea Press for assisting me with the manuscript, and take pleasure in giving special thanks to Aostra Hamman for her help with the references.

Art Acknowledgments

Page i: Calligrapher of Winged Heart: Hafizullah

Page iii: Werner Forman Archive, London: Arch, Jaisalmer, India

Page vii: The British Museum, London

Page viii: Reproduced by kind permission of the Trustees of the Chester Beatty Library, Dublin: CBL In. 07A.14. A Sufi Sage, by the Indian Painter Bichitr, Mughal School, 17th century

Page xi: The Metropolitan Museum of Art, Rogers Fund, 1935 (35.120) Photograph by Schecter Lee. Photograph ©1985 The Metropolitan Museum of Art, New York: Tombstone, of Mahmud, son of Dada Muhammad of Yazd, 1352, Marble.

Page xii (border): National Space Science Data Center, USA

Page xii top left: The British Museum, London

Page xii btm right: Bibliothèque centrale du Muséum national d'Histoire naturelle, Paris: P779 – Falcon-shaped calligraphy of a prayer, Persia, early 19th century.

Pages 1 (detail) & 7 top: Sonia Halliday Photographs, Aylesbury, UK

Page 2: The British Library, London: X.121 Plate XLV—"Bazar des Tailleurs, Ispahan"; Monuments modernes de la Perse, P Coste and E Flandin, Paris, 1865

Page 3: The British Museum, London

Page 5 top: Photograph: Yolande Crowe

Page 5 middle: The British Library, London

Pages 5 btm & 136 (detail): Reproduced by kind permission of the Trustees of the Chester Beatty Library, Dublin

Page 6: Werner Forman Archive, London

Page 8: Bildarchiv Preussischer Kulturbesitz, Berlin: KGM 1889,156 – Prayer Rug, Bursa Istanbul or Cairo, 16th century, wool and silk

Page 11: Photograph: Roland and Sabrina Michaud: Man praying at Ziyaratgah, near Herat

Page 13: Photograph: Yolande Crowe: Mosaic tile-work in the shrine of a poet and Sufi saint, early 15th century, near Herat

Page 16: Topkapi Palace Museum, Istanbul, Turkey

Page 17 top: Science Museum/Science & Society Picture Library, London

Page 21: Photograph: Nader Ardalan

Page 22: Photograph: Roland and Sabrina Michaud

Pages 27 (detail) & 184: The British Museum, London

Pages 28 (detail) & 29: Getty Research Library, Wim Swaan Photograph Collection, 96.P.21: Large Thuluth script decorating the central medallion of a dome in the mosque of Hagia Sophia

Page 42: The British Library, London

Pages 47 (detail) & 59: Freer Gallery of Art, Smithsonian Institution, Washington, D.C.: Purchase, F1946.12.153b

Page 48: Photograph: Christina Gascoigne

Page 54: Photograph: Roland and Sabrina Michaud

Page 66: The British Library, London

Pages 69 (detail) & 76: Bibliothèque nationale de France, Paris

Page 71: Photograph: Christina Gascoigne

Pages 72 (detail) & 90: The British Library, London

Page 74: The British Museum, London

Page 75: Photograph: Bastin & Evrard sprl

Page 78: The British Library, London

Pages 119 (detail) & 131: Bodleian Library, Oxford

Pages 91 (detail) & 125: Bodleian Library, Oxford

Pages 92 (detail) & 127: Egyptian National Library, Cairo, Egypt/Bridgeman Art Library

Pages 109 (detail) & 116: The Metropolitan Museum of Art, Rogers Fund, 1918 (17.81.4) Photograph ©1986 The Metropolitan Museum of Art, New York, USA

Page 112: Photograph: Josephine Powell

Pages 120 (detail) & 133: Bibliothèque nationale de France, Paris

Page 126: Bibliothèque nationale de France, Paris

Page 128: Bibliothèque nationale de France, Paris

Pages 139 (detail) & 140: The British Library, London

Page 143: Topkapi Palace Museum, Istanbul, Turkey

Page 146: Photograph: Professor Seyyed Hossein Nasr

Page 14: Werner Forman Archive, London

Page 153: The Keir Collection, London

Page 154: Reproduced by kind permission of the Trustees of the Chester Beatty Library, Dublin

Pages 157 (detail) & 174: Bibliothèque nationale de France, Paris

Page 161: Photograph: Roland and Sabrina Michaud: Man praying in the courtyard of the Karaouine Mosque in Fez, Morocco.

Page 164: Rijksmuseum, Amsterdam

Page 170: The Metropolitan Museum of Art, Gift of Alexander Smith Cochran, 1913 (13.228.39) Photograph ©The Metropolitan Museum of Art, New York

Page 172: Mary Evans Picture Library, London

Page 173: The British Library, London

Page 176 top: The British Library, London

Page 176 btm: The Sufi Order

Pages 177 & 183: National Space Science Data Center, USA

Page 178: Photograph: John Donat: Blue Mosque at Tabriz.

Page 179: National Space Science Data Center, USA

Page 180 top: Calouste Gulbenkian Foundation, Portugal

Page 180 btm: Adam Woofitt/Robert Harding Picture Library, London

Page 181 btm: John Martin, *The Last Man,* Laing Art Gallery, Liverpool

Page 182: The British Library, London

Page 185 top: National Space Science Data Center, USA

Page 185 btm: National Space Science Data Center, USA